Focus on Construction Contract Formation

Peter Aeberli

© Peter Aeberli 2003
Published by RIBA Enterprises Ltd, 1–3 Dufferin Street,
London EC1Y 8NA

ISBN 1 85946 110 7

Product Code 24880

British Library Cataloguing in Publications Data
A catalogue record for this book is available from the British Library

Publisher: Steven Cross
Commissioning Editor: Matthew Thompson
Editor: David Hawthorn
Project Editor: Anna Walters
Designed by: US2 Design
Printed and bound by Hobbs the Printers, Hampshire

While every effort has been made to check the accuracy of the
information given in this book, readers should always make their own
checks. Neither the Author nor the Publisher accepts any responsibility
for mis-statements made in it or misunderstandings arising from it.

Contents

Introduction to the series

This is the first of a series of books, written by invited authors who are authorities in the field. Each publication will focus on a topic that is frequently encountered during the course of a construction project. It will explain, in a manner accessible to a lay person, the relevant legal and technical principles concerning the topic and, using examples and illustrations, demonstrate their application to the day to day business of construction.

The series should be of interest not only to those completing their professional training but also to those who are responsible for the commissioning and running of projects. It should also be of interest to arbitrators and adjudicators, particularly those without a formal legal training.

Peter Aeberli MA(Edin), BA(Oxon). Dip Arch, DipICArb, FCIArb is a Chartered Architect and practising Barrister, Chartered Arbitrator, Adjudicator and Registered CEDR Mediator.

Introduction to *Focus on Construction Contract Formation*

This publication provides, in a manner accessible to those without any legal training or background, a practical understanding of the legal principles that govern the formation and validity of contracts and their implications for those engaged in the construction industry, whether as consultants, contractors or specialists. An understanding of these principles will enable those responsible for the commissioning of work to prepare and conclude effective contracts, and help to reduce the incidence of disputes that, however they start, end with an argument about what, if anything, was agreed between the parties and whether any agreement reached is effective in law.

Because this publication is intended for readers who do not have a legal training or background, no case law is cited and legal terminology is avoided wherever possible or, if used, is explained. For those who wish to consider the topics discussed in this publication in more detail, a list of references and further reading is given in Appendix 1.

1. Introducing contract law

See this chapter for:

- **an introduction to legal systems;**
- **the law of obligations;**
- **contract as part of the law of obligations;**
- **categories of contract;**
- **the importance of contracts in the construction industry;**
- **non-contractual provision of goods or services.**

1.1 Legal systems

A legal system, such as the law of England and Wales, can be viewed as a system for identifying factual situations where the state will impose sanctions on a person (**criminal law**), where one person can seek redress from another person (**civil law**), and where a person can challenge decisions of the state and public bodies, such as local authorities (**administrative law**). For example:

- If someone takes property belonging to another with the intention of permanently depriving them of that property, this is categorised by the criminal law as a **crime** (theft) for which the state can seek an order for imprisonment, a fine or both.
- The same conduct is categorised by the civil law as a **tort** (known as conversion) for which the person whose property is taken can seek an order requiring the person taking the property to return it, to pay compensation (damages), or both.
- If the property is taken by the state or a public body in wrongful exercise of a statutory or other power, the decision to do so can be challenged in administrative law by seeking a declaration that it is invalid and should be reconsidered.

1.1.1 Criminal, civil and administrative law

As can be seen from these examples, criminal, civil and administrative law can often be distinguished by the redress provided. The criminal law is principally concerned with the imposition of fines and imprisonment sought by the state against persons. The civil law is principally concerned with awarding compensation and making orders in favour of one person against another. Administrative law is principally concerned with making orders concerning the administrative actions of the state and public bodies.

1.1.2 Obtaining redress

The usual means of obtaining redress is in a court of law. The criminal courts, primarily the Magistrates' Courts and the Crown Court, are concerned with redress in respect of criminal matters. The civil courts, primarily the County Courts and the High Court, are concerned with redress regarding civil claims. In many countries, a separate court is established to deal with claims concerning the administrative actions of the state and public bodies, but this is not the case in England and Wales, where administrative law matters are dealt with by the High Court.

The courts are not the only means of obtaining redress in many civil matters. For example, commercial parties may prefer their disputes to be resolved in a private forum, such as through mediation or arbitration, rather than by the court, and under many construction contracts there is a right to adjudicate disputes. But, even in such cases, the court remains available to the parties to support and supervise the chosen method of dispute resolution.

1.2 The civil law of obligations

Each of the principal divisions of law – criminal law, civil law and administrative law – contains numerous subdivisions. The subdivision that is relevant to this publication, and to the series of which it forms part, is that part of the civil law concerned with the law of obligations.

1.2.1 Obligations in contract and tort

The law of obligations has, in turn, two parts: the law of contract and the law of torts.

- In the **law of contract**, a person's obligations are primarily founded on agreement and are, in general, owed only to the other party to the agreement, not to persons generally. Because obligations owed in contract are founded on agreement, they can be as prescriptive and detailed as the parties wish and their agreement requires. For example, agreed obligations can concern the development of an office block in accordance with detailed requirements, or the structuring of a long-term business relationship, such as a partnership. It would be impossible to regulate such relationships using only the law of torts, since obligations in tort are too generalised.
- In the **law of torts**, a person's obligations are primarily determined by general principles of law and are, ordinarily, owed to persons generally. Since obligations owed in tort are imposed as part of the general law, they are expressed in the form of general standards of conduct. For example: the obligation to exercise reasonable skill and care so as not to cause injury or damage to others forms the basis of the tort of negligence; the obligation not to unreasonably interfere with a person's use or enjoyment of their land forms the basis of the tort of nuisance.

Both parts of the law of obligations are significant for the construction industry. Work on a building project, such as the provision of consultant services, construction or materials, will ordinarily be carried out under a contract since this is the only way that obligations having the required definition and precision can be given legal force. But the work provided may, if defective, cause damage not only to the person with whom those obligations are agreed but to others, such as adjacent landowners, users and subsequent owners of the project. While the person or persons with whom the contract is made will, ordinarily, be able to seek redress in the law of contract, those who are not parties to that contract will have to seek redress in the law of torts.

The law of contract is of fundamental importance for the construction industry because the contract is the principal vehicle for those working on a project to be engaged, their obligations regulated and redress assessed if things go wrong. The law of torts has a subsidiary importance if things do go wrong.

1.2.2 Rights and obligations

Although the law is often discussed in terms of obligations, there is, in general, for each obligation a corresponding right. Thus, an obligation not to unreasonably interfere with a person's use or enjoyment of land can be seen, from the perspective of a landowner, as a right to enjoy and use their land free from such unreasonable interference. An obligation to perform the terms of an agreement can be viewed from the other party's perspective as a right to have those obligations performed. In contract law, these rights and obligations are often referred to as the **benefits** and **burdens** of the contract.

1.3 Defining a contract

There are various definitions that attempt to encapsulate the essential nature of a contract. The definition that is most readily understandable in a commercial context is that a contract is an agreement that gives rise to obligations, and corresponding rights, that the law will recognise and enforce.

This definition has important implications.

- Since a contract is founded on agreement, the parties are free, within wide limits, to agree the obligations to which they wish to be bound. This is known as the **doctrine of freedom of contract.** It means, at any rate in a commercial context, that the parties to a contract will ordinarily be bound by the agreement they make, however inappropriate, one sided or even ruinous that agreement may turn out to be for one of them.
- The corollary of the doctrine of freedom of contract is that a person cannot be forced to contract. In a commercial context this means that, if terms cannot be agreed, either party to the negotiations can walk away, however inconvenient or costly, in terms of wasted time and money, this is for the other party. It may be possible to break off negotiations and walk away even

if work has commenced in anticipation of a proposed contract.
- Once a contract is concluded, it binds the parties in law. If a
  party to a contract fails to comply with its obligations under
  the contract, the other can seek redress for that failure.
  This can be done, as appropriate, by enforcing a right to payment
  (a claim in debt), by seeking financial compensation for losses
  suffered as a result of the failure (a claim in damages for breach
  of contract) or, in certain circumstances where financial
  compensation does not provide adequate redress, by an order
  that the defaulting party perform its obligations (a claim for
  specific performance) or stop acting in breach of its obligations
  (an injunction). For example, if a consultant fails to perform
  services he or she has contracted to provide, the client can seek
  damages based on the additional cost of obtaining substitute
  performance from another consultant. If an employer fails to pay
  for work provided by a contractor, the contractor can recover
  that payment as a debt. If a person contracts to sell land, such as
  an office or house, but refuses to complete the sale, the
  purchaser can seek an order that the land be conveyed to it.

1.4 Categories of contract

Many of the legal principles within the law of contract, including
most of the principles discussed in this publication, apply generally
to all categories of contract. But there are a number of legal
principles, particularly those that make inroads into the doctrine of
freedom of contract, that only apply to specific categories of contract.
The categories of contract that are most relevant to the construction
industry include the following. The list is not, by any means, exhaustive.

- **Contracts made by deed and simple contracts** (the rest).
  Contracts entered into by deed do not require **consideration**;
  simple contracts do. For example, a promise of a gift will be
  contractually binding only if it is given by deed. Contracts made by
  deed also attract a longer limitation period (the period during
  which proceedings for redress must ordinarily commence) than
  simple contracts. The period is 12 years from breach for contracts
  made by deed, 6 years from breach for simple contracts.

- **Contracts for the sale of goods** (such as a contract for the sale of a motor car), for **work and materials**, also known as contracts for goods and **services** (such as a contract for building works), and for services (such as a contract to prepare designs). Contracts for the sale of goods are subject to an extensive statutory code governing matters such as the seller's obligations concerning the quality of the goods, the transfer of title in goods sold, and claims for defects and for non-delivery. This code is contained in Sale of Goods Acts, the principal Act being the Sale of Goods Act 1979, as amended. Contracts for the supply of services and for work and materials are governed by a somewhat more rudimentary code contained in the Supply of Goods and Services Acts, the principal Act being the Supply of Goods and Services Act 1982, as amended. This covers matters such as the supplier's obligations as regards the quality of any materials (goods) supplied and the standard of services (work) provided.
- **Contracts for estates or interests in land** (such as a contract for the sale or lease of a house or office). Such contracts are governed by the Law of Property Acts and related legislation and by that branch of the law known as the law of real property.
- **Construction contracts** as defined in the Housing Grants, Construction and Regeneration Act 1996, Part II. Most such contracts are subject to the code for payment and dispute resolution provided for in that Act.
- **Arbitration agreements** (an agreement that provides that disputes will be determined by a private tribunal sitting as arbitrator, not by the court). Such agreements are subject to the detailed code set out in the Arbitration Act 1996.
- **Consumer contracts** (certain categories of contract, principally contracts for goods, for work and materials and for services where one of the parties is contracting for purposes that are outside the scope of its business, if any, and the other is contracting in the course of a business). Such contracts are subject to various statutory controls that may invalidate certain types of unfair or unreasonable terms imposed to the determent of the consumer: for example, clauses that purport to exempt liability for death or injury, or which, not having been fairly

negotiated, exclude or restrict liability for defective performance. The Sale of Goods Acts and the Supply of Goods and Services Acts contain special provisions that apply only to consumer contracts for the sale of goods, the supply of work and materials and for services, not to contracts where both parties are contracting in the course of a business.

The same contract may come within a number of these categories and thus be subject to a range of different, possibly conflicting, legal principles. For example a contract entered into between a consultant and a small retailer for the design of a new shop is a contract for services and will, unless excluded, be subject to the implied terms provided for in the Supply of Goods and Services Acts. The contract may also be a consumer contract, since property development or refurbishment may not be regarded as an ordinary incident of the retailer's business, and be subject to the various statutory controls over any unfair and/or unreasonable terms imposed on the retailer by the architect. The contract will also be a construction contract as defined in the Housing Grants, Construction and Regeneration Act 1996, Part II and will be subject to the code for payment and dispute resolution provided for in that Act. A code that, since it favours the architect as the provider of services, over the retailer who pays for those services, might, but for its statutory force, be considered as unfair or unreasonable to the consumer, the retailer.

1.5 The importance of contracts in the construction industry

It should be obvious from the above discussion that the law of contract, the ability to agree legally enforceable obligations, is of fundamental importance to those engaged in the construction industry. It is only by forming agreements that are recognised as binding by the law of contract that the parties can regulate their rights and obligations in the knowledge that these rights and obligations can, if necessary, be enforced.

Given the importance of contract law in structuring commercial relations, it is surprising that those procuring and providing work in the construction industry often deal inadequately with the formation of their contracts. This leads not only to uncertainties about what was agreed and when, but also to disputes about whether a binding agreement was concluded at all and whether legally enforceable obligations are created to provide work or to pay for it. Such disputes can arise during the work as well as after it is completed.

This publication seeks to address this problem by providing those engaged in the construction industry, whether as employers, consultants, contractors or suppliers, with a lay person's guide to what must be done to agree legally binding obligations: what is necessary to conclude a valid contract.

1.6 Non-contractual supplies

There may be circumstances where a person supplies goods, work and materials or services to another, but the parties fail to agree a contract for that supply or the contract they agree is invalid. If so, the supplier will not be contractually entitled to payment for those goods or services and the purchaser will not be entitled to the supply or to a particular quality of supply. Nevertheless, if the envisaged goods or services are supplied, the supplier may be entitled to claim recompense for what is supplied under the doctrine of restitution (sometimes referred to, in this context, as *quasi contract*).

This means that where, in a commercial context, goods or services are supplied in response to a non-contractual request for those goods or services the supplier may be entitled to a reasonable sum for the goods or services supplied. This principle does not apply where there is an agreement or understanding that such work is to be provided free or at risk, for example where a consultant provides design ideas to a possible client in the hope of winning a commission.

If the supply is made under an invalid contract and it can be returned, as in the case of goods that have not yet been used by the buyer, it may be that each party will be required to return what it obtained from the other party – the buyer, the goods and the seller, the price.

The doctrine of restitution is also important where work is carried out under a **letter of intent**, a topic that is considered later in this publication.

2. Contract formation

See this chapter for:

- the requirements for a contract;
- offer, acceptance, and invitation to tender;
- consideration and intent;
- the need for certainty of terms;
- reaching and recording agreement;
- contract formalities and when they are necessary;
- when deeds are required and how they are made.

2.1 The requirements for a contract

The three principal requirements that must be satisfied to form a contract are **agreement, consideration**, and **intention to contract**; although, if the contract is made by deed, there is no need for consideration. In addition to these requirements, the persons between whom the contract is made (usually referred to as **parties**) must have sufficient **capacity** to contract, and the terms of the contract must be sufficiently **certain** to be capable of enforcement. Certain categories of contract must also comply with additional **formalities**, such as a requirement to be in writing, if they are to be valid.

2.1.1 Satisfying the requirements for a contract

In order to decide whether the requirements for a contract are satisfied, the parties' conduct up to the time that the contract is said to be concluded must be considered objectively (which means from the perspective of a disinterested bystander who does not know either party's intentions or motivations). If, from this objective standpoint, it can be inferred from the parties' conduct that the requirements for a contract are satisfied, they will, ordinarily, be found to have concluded a contract, irrespective of their private views about the matter.

2.1.2 Interpreting a contract

If the parties conclude a contract, it will be interpreted (construed)

11

objectively by reference to the words used in the contract considered in the light of the circumstances at the time the contract was made. The individual views of either party about what the contract meant or about how it was to be operated are, generally, irrelevant.

2.2 Agreement

The foundation of a contract is the parties' agreement to be bound by the terms of that contract. The ordinary test for deciding whether the parties have reached an agreement is to ask whether, objectively considered, an offer has been made by a person to another on the terms in question and, if so, whether that offer has been accepted by the person to whom it was addressed.

2.2.1 Making an offer

An offer is an expression of willingness to contract on certain terms made by a person with the intention that the offer will be binding on them as soon as it is accepted by the person to whom it is addressed. An offer is not effective until it is communicated to the person to whom it is addressed.

- An offer can be made to a single person, such as where an offer is made to carry out construction works for a developer, or it can be made to a class of persons, such as where a reward is advertised for the return of a lost pet.
- An offer can be made verbally, for instance during a telephone conversation or by leaving a message on an answering machine. It can be made in writing, for instance by letter or facsimile, or it can be made by conduct, for example by presenting goods taken from the shelves of a self-service shop at the checkout for payment.
- An enquiry about the price at which a person may be prepared to sell a particular item or perform certain services is not an offer; it is merely a request for information. Similarly, a request for further details about the terms on which an offer is made or about the goods or work to which it relates is a request for information; it is not an offer.

An offer should identify all the terms on which the maker proposes to contract, either by setting them out in the offer itself or by identifying the documents in which those terms can be found. This is because, once an offer is accepted, and a contract is made, its terms cannot be altered without a further agreement between the parties.

2.2.2 Inviting tenders

An offer is not the same as an invitation to make an offer (an invitation to treat, or to tender). Unlike an offer, an invitation to treat is not made with the intention that it will be binding on acceptance. It is made with the intention of inviting the person or, more usually, persons to whom it is addressed to make offers concerning the subject matter of the invitation.

- A useful but not infallible test for deciding whether words or conduct should be interpreted as an invitation to treat, rather than as an offer, is to ask whether, if the words or conduct are interpreted as an offer capable of immediate acceptance by all those to whom it is addressed, there is a possibility that more contracts will be made for the subject matter than can be fulfilled. Another useful test is to ask whether the person whose words or conduct are being considered did not intend to be bound until they knew the identity of the person with whom they were dealing.
- Examples of invitations to treat include invitations, for instance by an auctioneer, to bid for goods, invitations to tender for work, such as work on a construction project, displays of goods in a shop window, and advertisements to sell goods placed in a newspaper.

In certain cases, an invitation to treat may embody an offer. An invitation to submit tenders for building works may amount not only to an invitation to submit offers to carry out the works for a stated price, but also to an offer to consider conforming tenders in accordance with the procedures in the invitation to tender documents: for instance, that the lowest conforming tender will be accepted. This offer is accepted by submitting a conforming tender for the work, and the party inviting the tenders is contractually bound to consider the conforming tender in accordance with the procedures in the invitation to tender documents. In order to avoid such difficulties, it is usual to state in an invitation to tender that the employer reserves the right not to accept the lowest or any tender for the works or that considerations other than price will be taken into account in evaluating tenders.

2.2.3 Withdrawing an offer

An offer can, ordinarily, be withdrawn at any time before it is accepted. But, to be effective, the withdrawal must be communicated to the person to whom the offer was addressed.

- An offer can be withdrawn by words or by conduct. For example, an offer of work can be withdrawn by giving the work to someone else, but this will be effective only when the person to whom the original offer was addressed is told about or becomes aware that the work has been given to someone else.
- An offer is automatically withdrawn if the time stated for accepting it expires or, if no time for acceptance is stated, a reasonable time for acceptance has elapsed. A reasonable time depends on all relevant circumstances, such as the subject matter of the offer, the way in which it was communicated, and the commercial context. A reasonable period for accepting an offer to buy shares on a stock exchange will be significantly shorter than that available for accepting an offer to carry out building work.
- Even if an offer states that it will remain open for a specific period, it can still be withdrawn within that period, unless the promise to keep the offer open for the stated period is, itself, contractually binding. For example, the parties may enter into an agreement under which one allows the other a period in which to accept an offer for the sale of specified goods or land at a stated price. Such an agreement is known as an **option**. It will not be contractually binding unless it is supported by consideration or is made by deed.

If an offer is accepted before its withdrawal is communicated, agreement is reached. If the other requirements for a valid contract are satisfied, a contract will be concluded at that time. Subsequent communication of the withdrawal is ineffective.

2.2.4 Accepting an offer

An acceptance is an unqualified expression of assent to the terms of an offer by a person to whom the offer is addressed. Acceptance is, in effect, words or conduct amounting to a 'yes' in answer to an offer.

- Acceptance can, unless the offer provides otherwise, be by words, or conduct. Examples include signing written terms presented by a party, accepting delivery of goods that have been offered for sale, and commencing work in response to a request to do so on stated terms.
- If an offer specifies a particular method for acceptance, that method must ordinarily be used unless the person making the offer dispenses with that requirement.
- To be effective, acceptance must ordinarily be communicated to the person making the offer.
- There is an exception (known as the **postal rule**) to the requirement that acceptance be communicated. This applies where, considering matters such as the manner in which the offer was communicated, it is reasonable to send the acceptance by public post (which means the Royal Mail – not, for instance, a courier). If this is the case then, provided the acceptance is properly addressed and posted, it will take effect when it is posted, and this will be the case even if it is then delayed or lost in the post. The postal rule is easily excluded, for instance by stating in the offer that acceptance must be received to be effective.
- A response to an offer that attempts to change or augment its terms, a 'yes, if…' response, is not an acceptance. For example, an offer to supply goods at a stated price or on stated terms is not accepted by an order for their supply at a different price or on different terms.
- A request for more information about or for clarification of an offer is not an acceptance.
- An offer cannot be accepted after it has been withdrawn or, unless extended, after the time limit for accepting it has expired.

- An offer can be accepted only by the person to whom it is addressed. For example, an offer sent to James Architects Ltd cannot be accepted in his personal capacity by a Mr James, RIBA.

2.2.5 Rejecting an offer and making a counter-offer

An offer is terminated (killed) if it is rejected but, to have this effect, the rejection must be communicated to the person making the offer. Once rejected, an offer can no longer be accepted. If the person to whom an offer is addressed proposes alternative terms, this is both a rejection of the initial offer and a counter-offer.

For example, if a consultant's offer to provide services to a developer at a stated price is met by a counter-proposal from the developer that the services be provided at a different price, the original offer by the consultant is replaced by a counter-offer from the developer. The counter-offer can be accepted by the consultant, but the consultant's original offer can no longer be accepted by the developer.

- Rejection can be by words or conduct. For example, an offer to supply goods is rejected if the goods are obtained from someone else.
- A request for more information about or for clarification of an offer is not, ordinarily, a rejection of the offer. If the offer is not withdrawn, it remains open for acceptance whether or not the requested information is provided.

2.2.6 Communicating offers, acceptances and rejections

The need for offers, acceptances and rejections to be communicated means that, other than in the case of an acceptance governed by the postal rule, the offer, acceptance or rejection must be brought to the notice of the person concerned.

- In the case of written communications, notice is given when the communication is delivered to the person concerned, is delivered to someone, such as a receptionist, authorised by that person to accept communications, or is put through a letter box at that person's address. Once this has been done, it is usually irrelevant whether or not the communication is misplaced, is looked at or comes to the attention of the person to whom it is addressed.

- In the case of instantaneous communications, such as fax, telephone message systems and telex, it is likely that notice is given when the communication is correctly sent by that method, unless the sender is aware, for instance by an automated error system, that the communication has not been received. A person who uses such equipment accepts that it is available to receive communications on their behalf in much the same way that they accept that communications can be delivered by being posted through their letter box or handed to their receptionist.

2.2.7 Agreement in practice

It is possible, as in the case of a shop purchase, for agreement to be reached by a single exchange of offer and acceptance. But, in business dealings, it is more usual for there to be a period of negotiations during which, if the negotiations are successful, a consensus emerges about the terms of the proposed contract, this consensus being followed by agreement to those terms.

In order to avoid disputes about what was agreed, and when, it is good practice to clearly acknowledge, in some public way, that agreement has been reached. This can be done by signing a document setting out the agreed terms, by exchanging letters in which the agreed terms are identified, by approving a note of the meeting at which agreement was reached, or by a handshake.

In most business dealings this is simply a matter of good practice. But some professionals, such as architects, are required by the codes of conduct of their governing bodies to ensure that the terms on which they are engaged are properly recorded in writing. If they fail to do so, they may find it difficult to establish the terms on which they rely, if these are disputed.

If negotiations are not concluded with a clear acknowledgement that agreement has been reached, there is a risk of later disputes about what, if anything, was agreed. Such disputes are difficult and costly to resolve since it will be necessary to analyse the oral and written negotiations between the parties to identify, in sequence, each offer and counter-offer made and to establish whether it, in turn, was met by a rejection, a counter-offer or an acceptance by the other party. What often emerges from an analysis of this type is a series of invitations to treat, offers, rejections, requests for more information or clarification, and counter-offers, culminating, if agreement is reached, in an acceptance (whether by words or conduct) of the last offer or counter-offer on the table at the time. Once this point in what is referred to as the **'battle of forms'** is reached, subsequent negotiations between the parties are irrelevant, unless they culminate in acceptance of a later offer to vary the terms of the previously concluded agreement.

- A party who begins to supply work, or who begins to accept work following a chain of offers and counter-offers, will ordinarily be regarded as having accepted by conduct the latest offer or counter-offer by the other party at the time that the supply commences.
- If the supply or acceptance of work begins at a time when there is no offer or counter-offer on the table, for instance because the other party's most recent offer or counter-offer has been rejected, or many terms of the proposed agreement are still unresolved, it will not be possible to regard this as an acceptance by conduct. If there is an agreement, it must be found in the subsequent conduct of the parties.
- Analysis of the parties' negotiations may fail to reveal a last offer or counter-offer accepted, but show that the parties reached a consensus on the principal terms of the envisaged contract, and then conducted their relationship as if it was governed by the envisaged terms. If so, this may be sufficient to show that, at some unspecified point during their relationship, the parties agreed to be bound by those terms.

2.3 Consideration

An agreement will not ordinarily be enforceable as a contract unless it is supported by **consideration** given by each party to the agreement. Consideration is a legal term that embodies the notion of 'bargained for exchange'. It means that each party must, by their agreement, give or promise something of value 'in the eyes of law' in return for what is given or promised by the other party. If only one party provides consideration, the agreement is not contractually binding. Thus, if two parties agree that one will give money to the other, the only party providing consideration is the party that promises the gift. Since the intended recipient does not provide consideration to support that promise, the agreement is not enforceable as a contract.

- The consideration provided by one party does not have to be of fair value or equivalent exchange when compared with that provided by the other party. It is irrelevant whether one or other of the parties makes a good or a bad bargain, for instance by promising to pay too much or too little. It is irrelevant whether the consideration given by one party in exchange for something of value by the other, such as tenancy, is of only nominal worth, such as a peppercorn rent. Thus a promise by one party to give up a legal claim against the other provides consideration for the other's promise to pay a substantial sum in respect of that claim, even if the claim is of doubtful validity or no validity, at least where the party giving up the claim does not know that it is unfounded.
- Consideration must be a detriment to the party giving it or a benefit to the party to whom it is given. In many cases a promise, such as a promise to pay money or do work, will be both a detriment to the maker and a benefit to the recipient. Thus the parties to an agreement to provide goods or services for payment both provide consideration. If the other requirements for a contract are present, their agreement will be contractually binding.
- Consideration need not be both a detriment and benefit; either is sufficient. A promise by a person to provide services or goods, a detriment to that person, is consideration for a promise by another person to pay for that work, even if the latter will derive no benefit from the work because, for instance, under the agreement the work is to be done for someone who is not a party to the agreement (known as **a third person** or **a third party**).

- Each party to an agreement must give consideration for what is provided or is promised by the other party. To use a legal expression, 'consideration must move from the promisee'.
  For example, a promise by one person to pay another for goods that are not supplied by the latter, but by a third person, is not contractually binding. The person to whom payment is promised does not give consideration for the promise of payment because he or she provides nothing that is either a benefit or a determent in exchange for that promise. If, however, the person to whom payment is promised undertakes that the goods will be provided by the third person, the promise to ensure that the goods are provided, being a determent, provides consideration for the promise of payment.

- Consideration by one party to an agreement must be given in exchange for consideration by the other party to that agreement. If the consideration promised by one party has already been given (**past consideration**), it does not support the other party's promise. For instance, an agreement to pay for work that is complete will not, ordinarily, be contractually binding. Since the work is already done, it cannot provide consideration for the promise to pay for it.

- Consideration cannot, ordinarily, be provided by a promise to perform, or by performance of an existing legal duty. For example, an agreement to accept part payment of an undisputed debt in full discharge of the balance of that debt is not contractually binding. Since the debtor is already under a legal obligation to pay the debt in full, its promise to pay part of the debt does not provide consideration for the creditor's agreement to accept less than the full amount. If the agreement changes the manner in which the debt is to be paid, not just the amount to be paid, the debtor's promise to make payment in the new way will provide consideration for the creditor's promise to accept part payment in full discharge of the debt, and the agreement will be contractually binding. If, under an existing contract, the debtor's obligation is to pay a reasonable sum for the supply, or the creditor has a disputed claim against the debtor, the debtor's agreement to pay a specific sum for the supply or in discharge of the claim is contractually binding. Both parties provide consideration by giving up the right to contest what the actual value of the supply or amount of the claim should be.

- Similar principles apply where a debtor agrees to make an additional payment, over and above the agreed price, for the performance of existing contractual obligations. The creditor does not give consideration to support the promise of more money. The agreement to pay more will not be contractually binding unless an additional determent, such as giving up a disputed claim for additional payment, is provided by the party to whom money is promised, or some additional benefit, not envisaged at the time of the original contract, is provided to the debtor by the creditor's continued performance of its existing obligations.

Although a promise or agreement that is not supported by consideration given by both parties is not enforceable as a simple contract, it may be enforceable if it is made by **deed**. The additional **formality** involved in making a deed substitutes for the requirement of consideration.

2.3.1 Consideration in practice

The requirement that both parties to an agreement provide consideration is readily satisfied where the agreement concerns the supply of goods or services in exchange for payment. Since most commercial agreements are of this type, the requirement for consideration seldom causes difficulties.

There are, however, certain types of commercial arrangement where only one party provides or promises to provide something. For instance, under a collateral warranty the party providing the warranty promises the party to whom the warranty is given that it has performed, or will perform, its obligations under a contract entered into with a third person. Such a promise is not, of itself, contractually binding since the person to whom the warranty is given provides no consideration in exchange for it. In order to be contractually enforceable, the warranty must be made by deed, or the person to whom it is given must promise or give something, usually of nominal value, in exchange. This is why a collateral warranty often provides that the warranty is given in exchange for the promise of, or payment of, a specific, usually small, sum of money.

The need for consideration can also cause difficulties where the parties to an existing contract make a further agreement (a variation agreement) concerning the same subject matter.

- If a variation agreement involves both parties giving up rights under their existing contract, or concerns the compromise of claims made under that contract, it will be contractually binding since both parties provide consideration. For instance, if a client and consultant agree to terminate the consultant's appointment before all of the services have been provided and paid for, both provide consideration under the agreement to terminate the consultant's appointment. The client gives up the right to further services and the consultant gives up the right to further payment.
- If a variation agreement is made after one of the parties to the existing contract has performed all of its obligations under that contract, and its effect is to release the other party from its remaining obligations under that contract, the variation agreement will not be contractually binding, unless it introduces new obligations. The party obtaining the release does not give consideration for it. For example, if a consultant, having completed its services, agrees with the client to waive part of its fee for those services, the waiver is not contractually binding, since the client provides no consideration for that agreement. If the consultant's fee, or its amount, is disputed by the client, then the consultant's promise to forgo that fee, or part of it, is contractually binding since the client gives up those contentions in exchange for the consultant's agreement to forgo its fee in whole or in part.

2.4 Intention to contract

An agreement, even if supported by consideration, will not be contractually binding if, considered objectively, the parties' dealings at the time the agreement was made show that they did not intend their agreement to be contractually binding.

- In the case of commercial agreements, **intention to contract** will be assumed. This assumption is difficult to rebut unless the parties have clearly indicated that their agreement is not to be regarded as a legal agreement by, for instance, stating that it is to bind 'in honour only and not as a contract'.
- Intention to contract may also be rebutted where the agreement between the parties is merely a consequence of their existing legal obligations. If a purchaser of goods engages a carrier to collect the goods from the seller, the subsequent agreement between the carrier and the seller concerning the collection of the goods does not, ordinarily, create a contract between the seller and the carrier. The agreement between carrier and seller is a consequence of the carrier's contract with the buyer and of the seller's contract with the buyer. The seller and the carrier do not intend to create legal relations. It is for this reason that agreements reached between a contract administrator and contractor during the course of a construction project seldom give rise to contracts that are separate from the contract that is being administered.
- In the case of domestic arrangements, intention to contract will not be assumed. For example, a guest does not contract with their host by accepting an invitation to dinner. Neither is a parent's promise of pocket money in exchange for their child's good behaviour contractually binding. On the other hand, if a non-domestic agreement is made between members of the same family, such as an agreement to share winnings from lottery tickets purchased by one family member out of a fund to which all contribute, an intention to contract may be found.

2.4.1 Intention to contract in practice

The requirement that the parties to an agreement must intend to contract seldom creates difficulties in the case of commercial agreements, such as agreements for the supply of goods or services in exchange for payment. If such an agreement is not to be contractually binding this must be clearly stated in the communications leading up to and forming the agreement.

It is for this reason that parties negotiating a sale of land will ordinarily state in their correspondence that it is 'subject to contract'. The effect of these words is to make it clear that the parties do not intend a contract to come into being between them until a formal document is prepared and signed by both parties even if, prior to that date, all of the terms of their contract are agreed.

2.5 Certainty

An agreement will not give rise to a contract if it is too uncertain or vague in meaning to create enforceable obligations. For example, an agreement to acquire specific goods 'on hire purchase' is too vague to be enforceable as a contract. There are too many uncertainties surrounding what is meant by hire purchase. Similarly, an agreement between a client and consultant under which the consultant promises to provide a collateral warranty to a purchaser of the project will be unenforceable unless the actual terms of the collateral warranty are identified as part of the agreement. Considered in isolation, the expression 'collateral warranty' is too uncertain to give rise to an enforceable obligation.

In deciding whether an agreement is sufficiently certain in meaning, the legal knowledge of those preparing it will be taken into account. An agreement prepared by commercial persons will not be interpreted too strictly or examined with the rigour that would be applied to a document drafted by lawyers. A commercial agreement will be interpreted broadly and fairly. If it deals with the principal aspects of the parties' relationship, it will be contractually binding even if expressed in crude and summary form or if subsidiary matters are ignored.

- Apparent uncertainty may be overcome by **custom** or trade usage. Thus an agreement to engage an architect for a fee 'on the usual percentage' may, at the time when the Royal Institute of British Architects (RIBA) published recommended percentage fees for different types of project, have been sufficiently certain to be enforceable. But since the RIBA no longer publishes recommended fees, it is doubtful whether this would now be the case.
- Apparent uncertainty may be overcome by **implication of law.**

For example, if an agreement fails to provide a mechanism for determining the price to be paid for the goods or services to be provided, an obligation to pay a reasonable price may be implied by the Sale of Goods Acts or the Supply of Goods and Services Acts. Similarly, an agreement providing for 'arbitration in England' is sufficiently certain to be enforceable as an agreement to resolve disputes before an arbitrator rather than in court, because the Arbitration Act 1996 provides the necessary machinery for appointing the arbitrator and conducting the proceedings.
The scope for overcoming uncertainty by implication of terms is, however, narrow. It cannot be used to make a contract where the parties' agreement fails to deal with the principal aspects of their relationship.

- Apparent uncertainty can be overcome by giving effect to the terms agreed by the parties in the manner in which, objectively considered, they intended those terms to be understood.
  For example, if parties agree terms that are not applicable to their relationship, such as where a main contractor engages a subcontractor for building work on the same terms as the main contract, it will be assumed that the parties intend only the terms of the main contract that are appropriate to the subcontract relationship to be incorporated, with these being interpreted as if they had been rewritten to suit that relationship.

- Meaningless or contradictory terms need not make an agreement too uncertain to be enforceable as a contract. Such terms will, if possible, be ignored (**severed**). But if the consequence of ignoring such terms is to create greater uncertainty, or to leave important aspects of the parties' relationship unresolved, the whole agreement may fail for uncertainty.

- An agreement that is dependent on the subjective whim of one or both of the parties, such as an agreement to purchase property 'subject to a satisfactory survey being obtained', or an agreement to agree 'such terms as are appropriate', will, ordinarily, be too uncertain to be capable of enforcement as a contract. If such an agreement includes an objective requirement, for example 'all work shall be to the reasonable satisfaction of the architect', the agreement will be enforceable because the parties have agreed an objective procedure for determining the required standard.

- An agreement to agree terms at some time in the future
  (an **agreement to agree**) is too uncertain to be enforceable as a
  contract. For example, an agreement that one of the parties to a
  contract will procure a performance bond in favour of the other
  party to that contract, without specifying the terms of the
  required bond, is an agreement to agree such terms. Since it is
  not possible to identify the terms of the required performance
  bond or to compel the parties to agree such terms, the
  agreement to provide the bond will fail for uncertainty.

2.5.1 Certainty in practice

An agreement that sets out the basic parameters of the parties'
relationship, which usually means what is to be provided for what,
is likely to be sufficiently certain to be enforceable as a contract.
In the case of an agreement for goods or for services the minimum
is that the goods or services to be provided should be identified
together with the price to be paid for those goods or services,
or a means for calculating that price stated or implied.

Uncertainty can occur where an agreement provides that the parties'
relationship is to be governed by documents, such as a standard
form contract, without properly considering the suitability of those
documents for the parties' relationship.

- If a standard form contract is referred to in an agreement, but
  this form includes alternative or optional provisions, for instance
  about insurance and payment, or contains provisions that require
  additional information to be agreed by the parties, for instance
  identifying a period of construction, it is important that the
  agreement deals with these matters. If it fails to do so, and it is
  not possible to establish what the parties intended in respect of
  such provisions, they may be disregarded. If, in their absence, it is
  not possible to identify the principal elements of the parties'
  agreement, the whole agreement may fail for uncertainty.
- If a standard form contract referred to in the parties' agreement
  is not immediately applicable to the parties' relationship, for

instance the parties to a subcontract agree that their contract shall incorporate the terms of the main contract, it may be far from clear which provisions of the incorporated form are applicable to the parties' relationship and how these should be rewritten to suit that relationship. Although the resulting uncertainty is unlikely to invalidate the subcontract, it will add an unnecessary layer of uncertainly, complexity and cost to the resolution of disputes between the parties.

2.6 Contract formalities

Although, to avoid disputes about what was agreed, it is good practice for the parties or those advising them to record agreements, including agreements to vary existing contracts, in writing, there is in most cases no legal requirement to do so. Unless of a type to which additional formalities apply, a contract is enforceable irrespective of whether it is made by signing a document setting out all of its terms, by exchange of letters, by written offer accepted by conduct, or by oral agreement at a meeting or over the telephone.

2.6.1 When are contract formalities required?

There are a few exceptions where, in order to be effective or subject to a statutory regime, a contract must be concluded in a particular way, such as by deed, in writing or evidenced in writing. The most important of these exceptions (there are others) are as follows:

- A contract for the sale or other disposition of an interest in land, other than a short lease under three years, for instance a contract for the purchase of a freehold or a long lease of a house, must, to be effective, be made in writing signed by or on behalf of the parties.
- A document will not, at common law, be effective to create or transfer a legal estate in land, such as a freehold or lease, other than a short lease under three years, unless made by deed.
- Certain types of consumer credit agreement and hire purchase agreement must, in order to be valid, be in writing and must comply with the statutory formalities laid down in the relevant legislation.

- A promise to answer for the debt or default of another (often referred to as a **guarantee**), such as a performance or on demand bond, must, to be enforceable, be made or evidenced in writing signed by or on behalf of the person giving the guarantee (the **surety**).
- A construction contract will not be governed by Part II of the Housing Grants, Construction and Regeneration Act 1996 (the Act that seeks to regulate payment provisions in construction contracts and provides for statutory adjudication of disputes under such contracts) unless the express terms of that contract are set out or evidenced in writing.

It used to be the case that certain types of corporations could only contract by deed. But this rule, which never applied to registered companies, has long been abolished.

2.6.2 Deeds

A **deed** is a document (often referred to as an **instrument**), made in the required form, that creates or transfers, or confirms the creation or transfer of, an interest or right in property, for instance a conveyance of land, or, such as a contract, that creates a binding obligation on one or more persons.

Many of the technicalities surrounding the use and making of deeds have been abolished. Other than for the conveyance of land or creation of leases, deeds are now principally used to give legal effect to gratuitous promises that would otherwise be unenforceable for want of consideration, or, in the case of contracts, to attract a 12-year limitation period from breach for the bringing of claims, rather than the 6-year period that would otherwise apply.

2.6.3 Making a deed

An instrument made by an **individual**, by a **registered company** (in general, a private or a public limited company) or by an incorporated charity is a deed if it makes sufficiently clear on its face that it is intended by the person making it or the parties to it to be a deed, and it is validly executed as a deed by that person or by one or more of the parties concerned. The old requirement that an instrument had to be sealed in order to be a deed has been abolished.

- The intention that an instrument is to be a deed is most readily established if the instrument describes itself as a deed or if it states that it is executed or signed as a deed, but the necessary intention can be shown in other ways. Thus it is possible that sealing the instrument, the old method of creating a deed, will be sufficient to show the necessary intention, at least where there is no other reason for the instrument to be sealed.
- An individual executes a deed by signing it in the presence of a witness who attests the signature (by signing the deed as witness) and it is then delivered as a deed by that individual or by a person authorised to do so on its behalf. Alternatively, the deed can be signed on behalf of an individual. This is done by signing it at the individual's direction in their presence, and in the presence of two witnesses each of whom attests the signature of the person signing on behalf of the individual concerned.
- A registered company, or an incorporated charity, executes a deed by affixing its common seal to the deed or, irrespective of whether or not it has a common seal, the deed is expressed, in whatever form or words, to be executed by the company and it is signed by a director and the secretary, or by two directors, of the company, and the deed is then delivered as a deed by the company or by a person authorised to do so on its behalf.

For a partnership to execute a deed, each partner must sign the deed in the presence of a witness who attests his signature. Alternatively, the deed can be executed in this manner by one of the partners on behalf of the partnership, but only if that partner has been authorised by all of the partners, by deed, to execute deeds on their behalf.

An instrument made by a **corporation aggregate** (other than a registered company or incorporated charity), such as a local authority, or by a **corporation sole**, such as a Minister of the Crown or a bishop acting in their official capacity, is a deed if it makes clear on its face that it is intended to be a deed and it is sealed, validly executed and delivered by that corporation.

- In the case of a corporation aggregate, the seal must be that of the corporation concerned. For valid execution, it must be affixed to the instrument in the presence of both a permanent officer of the corporation, such as the secretary of the corporation, or such an officer's deputy, and of a member of the governing body of the corporation, for instance a member of the board of directors, and must be attested (signed) by them both.
- In the case of a corporation sole, it seems that the corporation's seal should be affixed to the instrument in the presence of the current holder of the office and attested by them in the presence of at least one witness, who should sign the deed as witness.

The requirement for a deed to be **delivered** does not mean that it has to be physically sent to the person in whose favour it is made. Any conduct that shows an intention to be immediately and unconditionally bound is sufficient to show delivery. For example if a deed includes words such as 'signed and delivered as a deed', this will be sufficient to show delivery.

A deed may be delivered **'as an escrow'**, that is conditionally. If so, it takes effect as a deed when the stipulated condition is satisfied. Once that condition is satisfied, the deed takes effect from the initial date of delivery, not from the date on which the condition is satisfied.

Although it is usual for a deed to be dated, this is not necessary since a deed takes effect on delivery.

2.6.4 Formalities in practice

The principal impact of contract formalities for those engaged in the construction industry concerns the requirement that the express terms of a contract must be recorded or evidenced in writing if that contract is to be subject to the statutory regime for payment and dispute resolution provided for in the Housing Grants, Construction and Regeneration Act 1996, Part II.

In practice, this requirement is not as onerous as it may seem since it is satisfied not only if the terms of the contract are set out in a document signed by the parties, but also if they are set out in documents referred to (**incorporated by reference**) in the exchange of correspondence forming the parties' agreement or in a letter of offer by one party accepted orally or by conduct by the other. It is even possible for this requirement to be satisfied where the parties conclude an oral agreement, provided that the oral agreement refers to documents in which all of the terms of their contract can be found or the oral terms are evidenced (recorded) in writing by one or other of the parties. It is important to ensure that any subsequent agreement to vary the original terms also satisfies these requirements.

This requirement for writing may not be satisfied if some of the terms of the parties' agreement are not reduced to, or evidenced in, writing – for instance, where agreement about outstanding matters is reached at a meeting and a contract concluded by handshake, but the agreements reached at the meeting are not then minuted or recorded in subsequent correspondence between the parties, only the fact of agreement. Such a contract, since it comprises a mixture of oral and written terms, may not be subject to the Housing Grants, Construction and Regeneration Act 1996, Part II.

The need to comply with formalities should also be borne in mind where the parties wish to contract by deed. The document prepared for signature should state that it is a deed, and the requirements concerning who should sign and how this should be done should be correctly observed.

The need to observe contract formalities is also important if guarantees, such as performance bonds, are required on a particular project, since, to be effective, these must be in writing or be evidenced in writing and signed by the person providing the guarantee.

3. Contract parties

See this chapter for:

- identifying the parties to a contract;
- capacity to contract;
- corporations and individuals;
- agency and assignment;
- the role of the contract administrator/employer's agent;
- privity of contract, and its exceptions;
- assignment, subcontracting and novation;
- warranties, duty of care letters and bonds.

3.1 The parties to a contract

The **parties** to a contract are the persons who have agreed to be bound by its terms and who have provided consideration for the promises it contains. The parties will usually be the persons whose communications result in the contract or those on whose behalf such communications are sent. For example, a building contract concluded between an employer and a contractor may provide that its terms are to be administered on the employer's behalf by a consultant. The consultant is not, however, a party to the contract as they have not given consideration for the promises made by the contractor. This is so irrespective of whether the consultant conducted negotiations leading to the contract on behalf of the employer. The parties are the employer, who provides consideration by promising to pay the contractor for its work, and the contractor, who promises to provide that work in exchange for payment.

3.1.1 Joint and several parties

If two or more parties to a contract promise to provide the same thing to another party to the contract, they both provide consideration and are **jointly** liable to the other party for the obligations owed under the contract. But performance by one joint party discharges the other. For example, if a client concludes a contract for design services with a partnership, all the partners at the time of the contract are joint parties to it. Performance of the services by one of the partners will discharge the others. But if performance is defective, all of the partners are jointly liable to the client under the contract for the resulting damage.

If two parties to a contract agree to provide separate things to another party to the contract, they are separately (**severally**) liable to provide what they have promised. Performance by one does not discharge the other. For example, separate (several) promises by two parties to a contract to pay a sum of money to the other party to the contract will be discharged only when each party giving a several promise has paid the sum it promised.

Contractual promises given by more than one party are presumed to be given jointly, unless the contract indicates otherwise.

3.2 Capacity to contract

A person can be a party to a contract only if they have sufficient capacity to contract. A person with capacity to contract is often referred to as a **legal person**. There are two categories of legal persons who have capacity: **individuals** and **corporations**.

3.2.1 Individuals

All individuals have full capacity to contract apart from minors, the mentally disturbed and the incapacitated. But individuals lacking full capacity to contract may still have a limited capacity to do so.

A minor is a person who has not yet reached their eighteenth birthday, the age of majority.

- A contract is not binding on a minor unless it is a contract for necessities and is beneficial to the minor in that it does not contain oppressive terms. Necessities include food, drink, clothing, accommodation, education and training that are appropriate to the minor's condition in life.
- A contract with a minor, other than for necessities, will bind the minor if the minor ratifies (affirms) the contract after reaching

the age of majority or, in the case of a contract for property having continuing obligations, such as a lease, if the contract is not repudiated by the minor within a reasonable time after reaching the age of majority.

- A contract with a minor is binding on the other party, if they have full capacity, and can be enforced against that party by the minor.

A mentally disturbed person is an individual who is mentally ill or disabled.

- A contract is not binding on a mentally disturbed person if it can be shown that, because of their mental condition, that person did not understand the transaction in question and the other party was aware of this. In the case of a contract for necessary goods, such as food and clothing, a mentally disturbed person is liable to pay a reasonable price.
- A contract with a mentally disturbed person binds the mentally disturbed person if they ratify (affirm) it during a period of lucidity.
- A contract with a mentally disturbed person is binding on the other party, if they have full capacity, and can be enforced against that party.

The principles governing the capacity to contract of persons incapacitated by drink or drugs are similar to those governing the capacity to contract of mentally disturbed persons.

3.2.2 Corporations
Corporations exist by statute, by charter or by common law.

- The most common type of corporation is the **registered company**, a company regulated by the Companies Acts. The corporate name of a registered company name will ordinarily include the designation Public Limited Company (plc) or Limited (Ltd). This name must be included on the corporation's correspondence and on its orders for goods and services.
- Registered companies are not the only kind of corporation. For example, most charities are corporations incorporated

under the Charities Acts, not under the Companies Acts. A professional body, such as the RIBA, or a university may be a corporation created by charter. An ecclesiastical office, such as a bishop, may be a corporation at common law.

- Most but not all corporations have a number of members, for example registered companies and charities. A corporation with a number of members is known as a **corporation aggregate**. Some corporations comprise an individual office holder for the time being and their successors; for instance, certain ecclesiastical positions in the Church of England. These are known as **corporations sole**.

Corporations have capacity to contract in their own right. A contract made by or on behalf of a corporation is a contract with the corporation. Neither a corporation's members nor its office holders for the time are parties to the contract. This is referred to as the **corporate veil**. It means that a corporation's members and office holders are not, ordinarily, liable for the debts incurred by the corporation in the course of its business.

Where a corporation is incorporated under statute, its capacity to contract is limited by that statute or by a constitution made pursuant to that statute. Such a corporation can only enter into contracts that are authorised by the relevant statue or by the objects clause in its constitution. Other than in the case of a registered company governed by the Companies Act, or a charitable company governed by the Charities Acts, contracts made by a corporation that are not authorised by the relevant statute or by its constitution are ***ultra vires*** and unenforceable by either party.

- The *ultra vires* rule has been largely abolished by the Companies Acts in the case of persons dealing with registered companies in good faith. Unless bad faith is shown, a person who contracts with a registered company is no longer at risk of that contract being invalid merely because it is not authorised by the company's constitution. An example of bad faith would be where a person contracting with the company was aware that the directors were concluding the contract for their own interests, not those of the company.

- Similar restrictions on the application of the *ultra vires* rule, to those that apply to registered companies, also apply in favour of persons contracting for full value with a charitable company if, at the time of contracting, they did not know that the contract was not authorised by the company's constitution or did not know that the company was a charity.
- The *ultra vires* rule does not apply, and never has applied, to non-statutory corporations, such as corporations created by charter or at common law.

3.2.3 Government departments and the Crown

The Crown, which includes the government and its departments of state, is an example of a non-statutory corporation sole. The Crown has capacity to contract, and its contracts are not governed by the *ultra vires* rule.

3.2.4 Public authorities

Public authorities are generally incorporated either by statute, such as local authorities which are governed by the Local Authority Acts, or charter, for example the British Broadcasting Corporation. If incorporated by statute, a public authority's contracts are governed by the *ultra vires* rule. A public authority's contracts must relate to its authorised functions. But, in the case of local authorities, the effect of the *ultra vires* rule is avoided where the local authority issues a certificate in the required statutory form stating that it has power to enter into the contract in question. In the case of contracts entered into with local authorities for construction work or for consultancy services relating to such work, such a certificate is seldom necessary since the procuring of such work is ordinarily part of a local authority's authorised functions.

3.2.5 Other organisations

Organisations, often referred to as **"unincorporated associations"**, that are neither individuals nor corporations do not have capacity to contract. The parties to a contract made with such an organisation will ordinarily be the person or persons whose communications resulted in the agreement giving rise to the contract or, if they authorised the contract to be made, the members of the organisation.

- A contract with an unincorporated association, such as a members' club, will ordinarily be made with all of the members of the club, or with all the members of its committee, or with the individual whose name appears on the relevant correspondence from that association. Which it is, in any particular case, depends on whether the contract was or was not authorised by the members or by the club's committee. If it was, the contract will be entered into jointly with all of the members or all of the members of the club's committee, as the case may be. If not, the contract will be entered into with the person whose signature appears on the club's correspondence.
- A contract with a partnership for the purpose of partnership business is, by statute, entered into jointly with all of the partners at the time of the contract together with any persons who hold themselves out as partners at that time, for instance by being listed as partners on the partnership correspondence.

If the name appearing on an organisation's business communications is neither that of an individual nor of a corporation, then that organisation is likely to be an unincorporated association or that name will be the trading name of an individual, a corporation or the partnership. It is the corporation or individuals trading under that name that are the parties to any contract concluded by the organisation.

3.2.6 Capacity in practice
It is important, when approached to do business with someone with whom one has not previously worked, to establish the legal person with whom one is dealing. This will, in any case, be necessary if financial checks are to be made of that person.

- Consider whether the approach is made by an individual in their own name or in the name of some other organisation.

An inspection of that person's correspondence should assist. If the only name identified on the letterhead is the name of the individual signing the letter the likelihood is that one is dealing with that individual.

- If the name on the letterhead is not that of the individual signing the letter, then it is likely that the letter is written by or on behalf of the organisation named on the letterhead. A similar conclusion can be reached if the individual writing the letter signs it over a name that is not his own, or words such as 'on behalf of...' appear below the signature.
- The name used in the letter may provide clues to the identify of the legal person on whose behalf the letter is written. If the name includes the designation Ltd or plc then the letter is written by or on behalf of a registered company of that name. The company is the legal person with whom one is dealing.
- If the name is not that of a registered company, then the letterhead and footer should be checked to see if that name is the trading name of such a company since, if this is the case, this should be stated. If the name is that of a registered charity, this should also be stated in the letterhead or footer.
- If, on inspection, it appears that the name of the organisation on whose behalf the letter is written is not an individual, a registered company or charity, or other corporation, then it is likely that the name is the trading name of a partnership, of an unincorporated association, or of an individual. If the name on the letterhead is that of a partnership this may be stated and the partners listed in the letterhead. But this is not always done.
- If it is not possible to establish the legal person with whom one is dealing from inspection of the correspondence, ask the writer of the letter on whose behalf the letter is written. If the necessary information is not provided, it may be prudent to decline the approach and look elsewhere for business.

3.3 Agency relationships

An **agent** is a person who acts for another (the **principal**) in a particular transaction or range of transactions, for example by entering into or performing a contract on the principal's behalf.

3.3.1 Creating an agency relationship

A relationship of **agency** is created between principal and agent by agreement, by conduct, or by statute.

- A relationship of agency is created by agreement where the principal agrees with the agent that the latter has authority to act on its behalf in a matter or type of matter: for instance where a client appoints a consultant to make a planning application, or enter into or administer a building contract on its behalf, or where an auctioneer is engaged by the owner of goods to sell those goods on its behalf. In such a case, the person appointed has express authority to conduct the business on the principal's behalf.
- A relationship of agency is created by conduct where the principal represents to those with whom the agent deals that the agent has authority to act on its behalf in a matter. This can be done either by putting a person in a position where others will assume that they have the necessary authority to do business on behalf of the principal (**implied authority**), or by advising such persons that the agent has the necessary authority (**ostensible authority**). For example, if a company describes a person as a contracts or sales manager, or a partnership identifies persons as partners on its letterhead, those persons have implied authority to contract on behalf of the company or firm concerned, even if they do not have express authority to do so.
- A relationship of agency can be created by statute. Thus, by the Partnership Acts, every partner in a firm is the agent of that firm and of the other partners for the purpose of the partnership business.

3.3.2 Contracts made by agents

If a relationship of agency exists, the agent's acts are those of the principal. Where an agent concludes a contract on behalf of a principal, it is the principal, not the agent, who is a party to the contract. The agent is merely the instrument though whom the contract is concluded.

- An agent should, ordinarily, advise those with whom they are contracting that they are acting as agent, even if they are not prepared to disclose the name of the principal. Provided that this is done, the contract will be formed with the principal, not the agent. If an agent, having the requisite authority, does not reveal that they are acting for a principal (known as an **undisclosed principal**), the person with whom the contract is made can choose (elect) whether to hold the agent or the undisclosed principal liable under the contract. Furthermore, in some circumstances, an undisclosed principal may not be regarded as a party to the contract at all and will not have any rights under it.
- If a person purports to conclude a contract on behalf of another person, without having that person's authority, they will be liable to the person with whom they purport to contract for **breach of warranty of authority**. But the person on whose behalf the contract was said to be concluded can, if in existence at the time of the contract, ratify the contract and thereby accept that it, not the agent, is a party. An undisclosed principal cannot ratify a contract made by an agent if, at the time the contract was made, the agent did not have authority to make that contract.
- Where a person concludes a contract on behalf of a company that is not yet incorporated, that person is liable under the contract. Since it was not in existence at the relevant time, the company is not a party to the contract and cannot ratify it.

3.3.3 The role of the contract administrator/employer's representative
Many standard form contracts require the employer to appoint a person to administer the contract on its behalf. The role of that person is determined by the contract under which they are appointed. There are two broad categories: the contract administrator, often described in the contract as the architect or the engineer; and the employer's representative.

- Where a contract administrator is intended, the contract terms will give powers and duties to that person, rather than the employer, but, the contract administrator is not a party to the contract. In some cases, such as when issuing instructions to the contractor, the contract administrator is the employer's agent and the employer is bound by the contract administrator's acts. In other cases, such as when issuing certificates for payment, awarding extensions of time or certifying practical completion, the contract administrator does not act as the employer's agent in this sense. Rather their role is to independently assess and give effect to the rights and obligations of both parties to the contract. The employer is not, in general, liable to the contractor if the contract administrator fails to perform this independent role properly, unless the employer has interfered with or prevented the performance of that role. When acting in this role, the contract administrator's decisions are only of temporary effect. Either party can ask an adjudicator, arbitrator or the court, as appropriate, to reassess their rights and obligations under the contract. The existence of a contract administrator's decision or certificate will not prevent this unless, such as in the case of a final certificate issued under many Joint Contract Tribunal standard form contracts, the contract expressly says otherwise.

- Where an employer's representative is intended, the contract terms will ordinarily refer only to the employer and the contractor. They will not mention the employer's representative. Instead, the contract will provide for the employer to name a person to act for it under the contract. Such a person is the employer's agent, and the employer is bound by and liable for the acts of its representative. An employer's representative, unlike a contract administrator, does not have an independent role.

A person appointed as a contract administrator or employer's representative does not have implied authority to alter the terms of the contact under which they are appointed. If, without the express agreement of the employer, they purport to do so, the employer will not be bound and they may be liable to the contractor for breach of warranty of authority.

3.3.4 Agency in practice
Questions of agency can arise when investigating the identity of persons with whom one proposes to do business. It may emerge in

the course of such investigations that the person with whom one is corresponding is acting as agent, not as principal. If so, the name of the principal should be established and, if unclear, the legal person who trades under that name.

Questions of agency can also arise if one is engaged to conduct business on behalf of another, for instance where a consultant is engaged by a client to obtain consents or procure goods or services from others for a development.

In many cases, the relationship of agency will be stated. Thus a consultant will ordinarily make clear in applications for consents that it is acting for a client. When inviting tenders for building works, a consultant will expressly state that it is doing so on behalf of a client, and the contract with the successful tenderer will, ordinarily, be executed by the client, not by the consultant as agent for the client.

Problems arise where the proposed relationships are not so clearly understood or are not confirmed in writing. For instance, if a consultant approaches their client for permission to engage a specialist to assist in a particular aspect of the design and, having been given permission to do so, engages that specialist, it may not be clear whether the specialist is in contract with the consultant or, through the agency of the consultant, with the client. This will depend principally on whether the client asked the consultant to engage the specialist on its behalf. If not, it is likely that the contract will be between the consultant and the specialist.

If, without the necessary authority, a consultant purports to contract with the specialist on behalf of the client, they may be liable to the specialist for breach of warranty of authority. On the other hand, if a client instructs a consultant to engage the specialist on its behalf, but the consultant does not advise the specialist that it is contracting on the client's behalf, the client will be an undisclosed principal and the consultant may be contractually liable to the specialist.

3.4 Privity of contract

A contract can, ordinarily, impose rights and obligations only on the parties to the contract, those who have given consideration for the promises contained in it. This principle, known as the doctrine of **privity of contract**, means that only the parties to a contract can enforce its obligations or be liable for non-performance of those obligations. This principle is, however, subject to a number of exceptions, the most important of which are as follows.

3.4.1 Assignment

A party's rights (often referred to as **benefits**) under a contract may, unless the contract says otherwise, be transferred by that party (the **assignor**) to a third person (the **assignee**), by agreement between the assignor and the assignee. Provided that the other party to the contract is given written notice of the assignment (a **legal assignment**), it must perform its remaining obligations to the assignee. The assignor is no longer entitled to the benefit of the performance. Even if the other party to the contract is not given written notice of the assignment (an **equitable assignment**), the assignee is, as between themselves and the assignor, entitled to the other party's performance. But, until notified of the assignment, the other party cannot be criticised for continuing to perform its obligations to the assignor.

In neither case can the assignee's rights under the contract be greater than those of the assignor. Thus, if the other party's performance is defective, any compensation payable to the assignee will be limited to what would, in the same circumstances, have been payable to the assignor.

As for the assignor's obligations under the contract, these will, despite the assignment, continue to be owed by it to the other party. Thus an assignment by an employer of its rights under a construction contract to a purchaser of the development does not release it from its obligation to pay the contractor for the work constructed both before and after the assignment.

3.4.2 Delegation and subcontracting

A party cannot transfer its obligations under a contract to a third person without the agreement of the other party to the contract (a **novation**). Obligations can, unless the contract says otherwise or it is a contract for personal services (such as a contract for the painting of a portrait), be delegated (**subcontracted**) to another person. But this does not relieve the contract party from its obligations under the contract. The contract party remains liable for their performance to the other party. For example:

- A builder who contracts to construct works remains liable under the contract for those works irrespective of whether it carries out those works using its own labour force or subcontracts the works, or parts of the works, to another.
- A consultant appointed by a client to provide designs for a development does not discharge that obligation by obtaining the necessary design information from others, such as a specialist contractor, even if the consultant exercises reasonable skill and care in selecting those from whom he or she obtains that design. The consultant remains contractually liable to the client for the design they have contracted to provide.

3.4.3 The Contracts (Rights of Third Parties) Act 1999

In the case of a contract entered into after 11 May 2000, the Contracts (Rights of Third Parties) Act 1999 (the 1999 Act) provides that a person who is not a party to that contract (a **third party**) may enforce a term of that contract if the contract expressly provides that it may do so, or the term purports to confer a benefit on the third party and the contract does not indicate that the parties did not intend that term to be enforceable by the third party. In either case, such a third party can enforce the term only if they are expressly identified in the contract by name, or as a member of a class, or as answering to a particular description. For example:

- If, in a contract between an employer and contractor, the contractor warrants to any purchaser of the project from the employer that the contract has been performed in accordance with its terms, such a purchaser could claim redress from the contractor if its contract with the employer is not properly performed. This is because the warranty purports to confer a benefit on a person answering to a particular description, the purchaser, and there is nothing in the contract to indicate that the employer and contractor did not intend the warranty to be enforceable by a purchaser of the development.

• If a client appoints a consultant to prepare designs for leasehold premises under a contract that identifies the freeholder by name or designation, it may be that the contract will be interpreted as being for the benefit of the freeholder as well as the client. If so, the freeholder may argue that it is entitled, under the 1999 Act, to enforce the contract in so far as the consultant's designs have affected the freeholder's interest in the premises.

It is possible to state in a contract that it is not intended to confer rights on third parties under the 1999 Act. This is commonly done in standard form construction contracts and consultant's agreements in order to minimise the risk that they might unintentionally confer rights on third parties.

3.4.4 Novation

A **novation** is an agreement by which an initial contract between two parties is rescinded and replaced by a new contract concerned with the same obligations but made between one of the original parties (the continuing party) and a new party. The effect of the novation is that the new party is substituted for and takes on the rights and obligations of the original party it replaces. In a true novation, the replaced party is released from all obligations to the continuing party and the continuing party is released from all of its obligations to the replaced party.

A novation can only occur with the agreement of all three parties concerned. For example, if a client wishes to novate its contract with a consultant to a design and build contractor, it must obtain the agreement of both the consultant and the design and build contractor.

In practice true novations are rare, at least where the initial contract has been partly performed. This is because the party that is to be replaced may be reluctant to give up its rights against the continuing party in respect of that performance. Hybrid arrangements where, after the novation, the continuing party has residual obligations to the replaced party as well as obligations to the new party are quite common. These residual obligations may either be referred to in the novation agreement itself or provided for by a separate warranty entered into between the continuing party and the replaced party.

3.4.5 Privity in practice
The doctrine of privity of contract generally serves those who supply goods or services in the construction industry well, since it limits the obligations for that supply to those with whom the contract is formed. Proposed contract terms should be checked for any indication that they confer rights on persons who are not parties to the contract. If so, the additional risk should be removed by excluding the operation of the 1999 Act, or it should be allowed for, for example in the price, and advised to insurers, if any.

Proposed contract terms should be checked for any indication that the rights or obligations under the contract will be transferable to others. If the terms are silent about these matters, either party will be able to assign its rights under the contract, but neither can be forced to agree a novation. If novation is proposed, the details of what is envisaged should be checked to see whether it is a true novation or a hybrid under which the continuing party, usually the supplier of goods or services, will have residual obligations to the replaced party, usually the client, after the novation.

A hybrid novation can lead to difficulties because the continuing party will in effect be serving two masters, who may have quite different expectations about what is required from it. For example, a consultant whose contract is novated from a developer to a design and build contractor, but who continues to have residual obligations to the developer, may be faced with a conflict of interest if it considers that the contractor's instructions to minimise design quality so as to maximise the contractors' profit (or reduce its loss) are at odds with the developer's aspiration for a high-quality development.

Where it is proposed to obtain information from others to assist in the performance of contractual obligations, for instance where a consultant appointed by a client to produce designs for a development wishes to rely on design information from specialists, consideration should be given to how contractual responsibility for that information is to be structured. There are a number of possibilities.

- The consultant can agree with the client that the person providing the information will be engaged under a separate contract with the client, and that the consultant will not be responsible for the information provided by that person. Where the person providing the information is a consultant, this is usually done by the client appointing that consultant to provide the required information. Thus an architect may agree with its client that an acoustic engineer should be appointed to deal with a particular aspect of the design.
- Where the person providing the information is a specialist contractor, there may be a reluctance to engage it before construction starts. If so, one arrangement commonly used is to require the main contractor, when appointed, to engage the specialist as a subcontractor for the construction of the work to which the information relates, but to oblige the specialist to give a warranty to the client concerning the adequacy of any design information provided. In the standard form contracts produced by the Joint Contracts Tribunal, this procedure is known as **nomination** or **naming** of a subcontractor. This relationship may cause difficulties, particularly where the required design information is not provided until after the main contractor is engaged. In such a case, there is a risk of delay and disruption of the main contractor's works due to delay in the provision of that information, and its acceptance by the consultant, these being matters for which the main contractor is not, ordinarily, responsible.
- The consultant can enter into a legal relationship with the person providing the required information so that, if the

information is defective and the consultant is held liable to the client, it can seek to recover its losses from the person who provided that information. Ideally, this will be done by subcontracting with the person concerned for the provision of the information and paying
for it. But a consultant may be reluctant to do this where the person concerned is a specialist contractor who, it is assumed, will be remunerated for the information it provides if engaged by the main contractor to carry out the work to which the information relates. In such a case the consultant may seek to obtain a **duty of care letter** from the specialist.

- The consultant can accept the risk that it, alone, will be liable if the information it obtains is defective, but seek to minimise that risk by ensuring that the information is obtained from a reputable source and is properly reviewed before it is used by the consultant.

3.5 Collateral arrangements

Although desirable from the perspective of those supplying goods and services, privity of contract can be inconvenient for those who might suffer loss if the supply is defective. This is a particular concern in the construction industry because such losses can be significant and may be incurred not just by the client but by those who fund, purchase or lease a development.

3.5.1 Types of collateral arrangements

Various types of collateral arrangements have developed for dealing with these concerns.

- A **collateral warranty** or **duty of care letter** is used to extend the number of persons to whom a supplier of goods and services is potentially liable beyond the party with whom it contracts, thus ensuring that those who may suffer a loss if the supply is defective can seek compensation from the supplier.
- A **bond** is used to ensure that, if the supply is defective, those who are entitled to compensation will be recompensed even if the supplier is insolvent.

3.5.2 Collateral warranties

A collateral warranty is a contract under which one party
(the **warrantor**) undertakes (**warrants**) to the other that it has
performed or will perform the obligations it owes to another
person (the **principal**) under a separate contract (the **principal
contract**) in accordance with the terms of the principal contract.

Despite the coming into force of the Contracts (Rights of Third
Parties) Act 1999, collateral warranties remain the principal vehicle
in the construction industry for providing persons, such as funders,
purchasers or major tenants, who might suffer loss if work on a
project is defective, with contractual rights against those
responsible for the work. Collateral warranties are also used to
give clients contractual rights against subcontractors and specialists
who are responsible for principal elements of the work, so as to
ensure that compensation for defective performance can be
recovered directly from the subcontractor or specialist in the event
of main contractor insolvency.

* A consultant may be required to provide a collateral warranty to
  a purchaser of the development on which it has supplied services
  warranting that it has properly performed the services supplied
  under its appointment from the client. If the consultant's services
  are defective then it will be liable to compensate both the client
  and the purchaser for the damage they have suffered: the client
  under the appointment, the purchaser under the warranty.
* A specialist subcontractor may be required to provide a collateral
  warranty to the employer on a project where it is to provide a
  major element of work, warranting that it will properly perform
  its subcontract with the main contractor. If the specialist's work
  is defective then both the employer and the main contractor will
  be able to claim compensation from the specialist for the
  damages they have suffered: the main contractor under the
  subcontract, the employer under the warranty.

Since a contractual warranty is collateral to the principal contract,
it should not, ordinarily, impose obligations on the warrantor that

are greater than those that it has accepted under the principal contract. In practice, additional obligations, such as an obligation to ensure that specified deleterious materials are not used, are not uncommon, and provided the risk is recognised, priced for and, if relevant, accepted by insurers, they create few problems. More invidious are provisions in collateral warranties that oblige the warrantor to indemnify the other party against damage caused by any failure to properly perform its obligations under the principal contract. Since the right to recover compensation on an indemnity arises when damage is suffered, and this may be many years after the principal contract is performed, the effect of such a clause is to create a significantly longer period of potential liability than the six or twelve year limitation period that will apply to claims under the principal contract. Provisions of this type should not be accepted in a warranty.

3.5.3 Duty of care letters

A more informal, and thus less certain, form of warranty may be sought by way of a **duty of care letter**. The substance of such a letter is that the writer, who will ordinarily be a supplier of goods or services, makes statements about the quality of the goods or services it is to supply or has supplied. These statements may, in the case of services, be to the effect that the supply will be, or has been, carried out with skill and care or, in the case of goods, that they will be or are suitable for the purposed use or will perform in a particular way.

The problem with such letters is that it may be difficult to show that consideration has been given for the promise they contain, particularly if the goods or services have already been supplied, or to establish the necessary intention to contract. If these requirements are not satisfied such letters will not have contractual force.

Even if such letters do not have contractual force, they may still give rise to a duty of care in negligence. For this to be the case, it must be shown that the writer knew or ought reasonably to have known that the letter would be relied on by a particular person, or a member of a particular class of persons, for a particular purpose, and that it was reasonable for the recipient to rely on the letter in the way that it did. But only a duty in negligence is limited to the exercise of skill and care in making the statements contained in the letter – a significantly less onerous duty than would be owed under a collateral warranty, particularly where the person providing the letter is providing goods or work and materials, not merely services.

3.5.4 Comfort letters

Comfort letters may be written in the context of complex contractual negotiations, where one party is concerned that the costs it is incurring in the negotiations, for instance by having to produce detailed cost or design information, may be wasted if the project does not proceed. The purpose of a comfort letter is to provide reassurance that such costs will not be wasted on a fruitless exercise. Even if such a letter is provided, it is likely to be meaningless. For example, if the letter states that the current policy is to meet the costs incurred by the recipient if the project is abandoned, this may be read merely as a statement of present policy, not as a promise that the policy might not change. If interpreted in this way, the letter is unlikely to give rise to a contract or provide a basis for recovery if the project is abandoned.

3.5.5 Bonds and guarantees

A bond, or guarantee, is a contract under which one party (the **guarantor** or **surety**) promises to the other (the **beneficiary**), to accept responsibility for another person's (the **principal's**) obligations to the beneficiary under a separate contract (the **principal contract**) entered into between the principal and the beneficiary. The primary purpose of such an arrangement is to provide the beneficiary with assurance that, if the principal defaults under the principal contract, a sum of money will be available from a financially secure source, such as a bank or insurance company, to compensate the beneficiary for that default. In most cases, the responsibility accepted by the surety is expressly limited to a maximum amount, often calculated as a percentage of the amount payable under the principal contract.

3.5.6 Performance bonds and on demand bonds

Two types of bond are commonly written in the construction industry, **performance bonds** and **on demand bonds**.

- A **performance bond** provides that the surety will be liable to pay the beneficiary sums up to the value of the bond only if, on a demand (a call) being made, it can be shown that the principal is in breach of the principal contract and that the beneficiary has suffered loss as a result of that breach in the amount claimed from the surety.
- An **on demand** bond provides that the surety is liable to pay the beneficiary amounts up to the value of the bond, only if a demand (a call) for that amount is made in the way required by the bond. It is not necessary to do more than this, for instance to prove that the principal is in breach of the principal contract and that the beneficiary has suffered loss as a result of that breach.

Performance bonds are usually provided by insurance companies on payment of a premium by the principal, the cost of which is likely to be passed on to the beneficiary under its contract with the principal. Since the insurance company will be out of pocket if it has to pay money to the beneficiary under the bond (if the bond is called), it will be concerned, before paying the amount demanded, to ensure that there has been a breach of the principal's contract with the beneficiary and that the beneficiary has suffered loss as a result of that breach.

On demand bonds are usually provided by the principal's bank, but only if the principal is able to provide assets (such as cleared funds in an account, or charges on property) from which any sums paid out under the bond can be recouped by the bank. Since the bank will not be out of pocket if the bond is called, it is not concerned, other than in the case of fraud, with the merits of claims under the principal's contract with the beneficiary. The bank is concerned only with whether the correct paperwork has been presented to it for calling the bond. The principal will be concerned, since it will be out of pocket if the bond is called, but, ordinarily, this is not the bank's concern.

3.5.7 Collateral arrangements in practice

A party to a contract cannot be obliged to enter into warranties or provide bonds unless stipulated for in its contract. The need for such arrangements must be considered before the contract is concluded and the necessary requirements, identifying the forms to be used, any entries required in those forms, and the persons to whom warranties or bonds are to be given, included as terms of the contract. In deciding what is appropriate, the different purposes of bonds and warranties should be born in mind. The possibility of creating rights for third parties through the Contracts (Rights of Third Parties) Act 1999, rather than by the use of warranties, should not be overlooked.

If asked to give warranties, the proposed terms should be considered and checked with insurers, if any. The risks associated with unusual provisions should be assessed and allowed for, or such provisions removed.

The wording of proposed bonds should also be reviewed and the possibility of obtaining the required bonds, and the costs of doing so, checked with insurers or banks as appropriate.

If a duty of care letter is proposed, the reasons why this is considered appropriate, rather than a collateral warranty or other contractual arrangement, such as a subcontract, should be evaluated. If the letter is intended to create legal obligations this should be made clear and the wording agreed between the parties concerned. In practice such letters are often requested to provide assurance where there is a concern that things may have already gone wrong. If provided at all in such circumstances, the wording of such a letter is likely to be vague and its legal significance obscure.

- If the letter is requested by a consultant from a specialist or other designer concerning information that the consultant requested them to provide, the purpose is likely to be to create a potential chain of liability should that information be defective. Is this acceptable and, if so, why should the specialist or designer not be paid for the information it is providing under a properly structured contract?

- If the letter is requested by someone with whom one is already in contract, such as where a client requests written assurance from a consultant or contractor that its services or work have been properly performed, the purpose is either to create an additional liability to the client beyond that owed under the contract or to create a potential liability to those, such as purchasers of the development, to whom the letter is shown. Before such a letter is written, it should be reviewed with insurers, if any. If the anticipated risks are not acceptable, the letter should not be provided or, if provided, should make clear that it is not intended to create additional liabilities beyond those already owed to the client.

4. Contract terms

See this chapter for:

- **the difference between express and implied terms;**
- **incorporating terms by reference;**
- **grounds for implying terms;**
- **typical implied terms in construction contracts;**
- **controls over exemption clauses.**

4.1 The parties' obligations under a contract

The obligations that the parties accept when they conclude a contract are contained in its terms. The terms may be **express** or **implied** or, more usually, a combination of both.

4.2 Express terms

Express terms are those that the parties expressly state when making their contract. Express terms may be written or oral. Oral terms may be evidenced in writing.

- Written terms may be set out in documents forming the contract – for example, where a client and builder execute a copy of a standard form building contract, such as a copy of the JCT Minor Works Agreement, setting out all of the terms they have agreed, or where, as is often the case in a contract for the sale of goods, all of the terms are set out in a letter of offer, accepted by the purchaser orally or by conduct.
- Written terms may be contained in documents referred to (**incorporated by reference**) in the exchange of communications forming the contract – for example where a client signs a copy of a consultant's appointment letter which states that the appointment is on the terms of the RIBA conditions CE/99, or where an appointment on those terms is agreed over the telephone.
- Oral terms may be agreed at a meeting or over the telephone. It is preferable for oral terms to be recorded (**evidenced**) in

writing so that there can be no dispute about what was said, for instance by making and circulating a note of what was agreed. But failure to do this will not affect the validity of such terms, unless the contract is of a type whose terms must be made or evidenced in writing.

4.2.1 Incorporating express terms by reference

If a party wishes to contract on terms contained in documents that are to be incorporated by reference, rather than on terms set out in an offer letter or other document to be signed by the parties, particular care must be taken to ensure that those terms are properly brought to the notice of the other party.

- In the ordinary case a party does this by identifying the relevant document in its letter of offer, making it clear that the document contains contract terms and stating where a copy can be found. If this is not done, the terms may not be incorporated. For example, if a contract is concluded by delivery of goods requested by written order, terms set out on the back of the order may not be incorporated if they are not referred to on the face of the order. If the order says that it is subject to terms overleaf, those terms may not be incorporated if the order is sent by fax, since there will be no terms on the back of the fax. Similar problems can occur where the reference to the document in which the terms are to be found is unclear or ambiguous. For example, if a consultant's appointment letter states that the appointment is on RIBA terms, this may be too vague to incorporate any particular standard terms published by the RIBA. The RIBA publishes a number of standard form consultant agreements, and it may not be possible to establish with sufficient certainty which standard form is meant. If the appointment letter states that the architect will work in accordance with CE/99, this may only be sufficient to incorporate the schedule of services, the Work Stages, included in that standard form, not the full terms, particularly if there is no other indication that these were to apply.
- Terms incorporated by reference should be appropriate to the

parties' relationship without amendment. Where a standard form contract is referred to, the form should be of a type that the parties could execute to conclude a contract: a main contract form for a contract between client and builder; a subcontract form between builder and subcontractor; a professional services agreement for a contract between client and consultant.

- Inappropriate forms are sometimes incorporated where, for instance, it is intended that a party's obligations under the contract, such as a contract between a contractor and subcontractor, should mirror the other party's obligations under a separate contract with a third person, such as a main contract entered into between the contractor and its employer. In such cases, it is stated that the terms of the subcontract are to be the same as those of the main contract (a **back-to-back arrangement**). This creates difficulties where the terms designed for one relationship do not suit the other. Thus the terms of a contract between an employer and contractor, particularly one that provides for a contract administrator appointed by the employer, will not suit, without extensive amendment, the relationship of contractor and subcontractor. The process of deciding what terms were intended to be incorporated by such words and how they were to be amended creates uncertainty and adds an additional layer of complexity and cost to any dispute concerning the contract.

- A further difficulty can occur where the document incorporated by reference contains terms, such as an arbitration clause, concerned with the resolution of disputes. If the dispute resolution clause is applicable, without amendment, to the parties' relationship, then it is likely to be regarded as a term of their agreement. For instance, where a contract between contractor and employer incorporates, by reference, the terms of the JCT Minor Works Agreement, the contract will incorporate all the terms of that standard form including the dispute resolution clauses, because the JCT Minor Works Agreement is designed for such a relationship. But if the dispute resolution clause in the incorporated document is not applicable to the parties' relationship, without amendment, it will probably not be incorporated unless expressly referred to along with the document in which it can be found. For example, if a contractor engaged under the JCT Minor Works Agreement subcontracts work on terms that state that the subcontract will be on the same terms as the main contract, the arbitration clause in the JCT Minor Works Agreement may not be incorporated into the subcontract, unless express words of incorporation, such as 'including the arbitration clause', are added.

4.2.2 Express terms in practice

Except in those few cases where a contract is governed by formal requirements, there are no restrictions on how express terms can be agreed. They may be set out in a written offer; they may be contained in documents, such as a standard form contract, referred to in that letter; some may be agreed orally in telephone conversations or at meetings at which the written offer is considered; others may be recorded in notes taken at a meeting where the contract was concluded. But such a proliferation of the sources of terms is not desirable. It increases uncertainty and the risk of disputes about what was agreed.

Ideally, all of the terms should be recorded in writing in a document signed by the parties, or the documents containing the terms should be listed in a letter that, when agreed by the other party, will form the contract. If the listed documents contain dispute resolution clauses these should be highlighted, particularly if the party to whom those terms are proposed is unfamiliar with such documents or the dispute resolution procedures they contain, such as where a consultant is appointed by a client who is not in business as a developer.

If terms are agreed at a meeting, or on the telephone, a note should be made of what was agreed, and circulated to the parties. If the contract is not concluded at that time, the note should be identified, along with the other documents in which the terms are set out, in the letter by which the contract will be concluded. If a contract is to be executed by the parties, the contract documents should be amended, before signing, to take account of the terms referred to in the note.

4.3 Implied terms

Implied terms are those that are included in a contract even if the parties do not expressly refer to them at the time the contract is concluded.

- Contract terms may be implied by law or by statute if the contract is of a type in which such terms are ordinarily implied and the implication of those terms is not contrary to the express terms of the contract. For example, terms are ordinarily implied by the Sale of Goods Acts into contracts for the sale of goods, and by the Supply of Goods and Services Acts and law into contracts for work and materials or for services.
- Terms may be implied to reflect the parties' presumed intention if, having regard to the words used in the contract and the circumstances at the time it was concluded, they are necessary to give business efficacy to the contract or are so obviously a part of the contract that both parties would, if asked at the time, have said that they go without saying. For example, a contract to use a wharf will be subject to an implied term that it is safe for the ship to lie at that wharf. But a term will not be implied on this basis if it is inconsistent with the express words of the contract.
- Terms may be implied by **custom** where the custom is a certain and general incident of a particular trade or place, and the use of the term is well known, reasonable and not contrary to law or to the express words of the contract. Thus, at a time when the only architects' standard form appointment was the RIBA Blue Book, it was arguable that there was a well-understood and accepted custom that architects contracted on those terms. This is no longer the case since not only does the RIBA publish a variety of appointments but it is no longer the only body that publishes consultants' agreements.
- Contract terms may be implied by course of dealing where

the parties have contracted on the same terms on a number of previous occasions and they make another contract of similar type without expressly referring to those terms.

Apart from terms that are implied by statute or law as normal incidents of particular types of contract, such as those implied into contracts for goods, for work and materials or for services, terms will not be readily implied, particularly where the parties have entered into a contract on standard or other terms that have been carefully drafted to cover all aspects of their relationship. Neither should it be assumed that, because a contract fails to deal expressly with a matter that is important to one of the parties, the omission will be cured by an implied term. A term will not be implied merely because it would improve the contract or because one or other party would have regarded it as desirable. A term will be implied only if it is necessary to make the contract work as, objectively considered, both parties must have intended.

4.3.1 Implied terms in practice

In the case of contracts entered into by those involved in the construction industry, implied terms such as the following are likely to be found unless excluded by the contract, or if the matters that the implied terms concern are expressly covered by the contract.

The principal implied terms concerning the quality of what is sold or supplied are as follows.

- A contract for services, such as a consultant's appointment, is ordinarily, subject to implied terms that the services will be performed with reasonable skill and care and in a reasonable time. There is no implied term that the work produced, for instance designs for a building, will be fit for the intended purpose.
- A contract for work and materials is, ordinarily, subject to similar implied terms concerning the work supplied, as a contract for services.
- A contract for work and materials is, ordinarily, subject to an

implied term that materials supplied under the contract will be of satisfactory quality. Satisfactory quality is concerned with whether the materials are sufficiently durable, are safe and are reasonably suitable for the purposes for which goods of that description and price are commonly supplied. If the materials are supplied for a particular purpose that has been made known to the supplier, there is a further implied term that they will be fit for that purpose unless the purchaser does not rely, or it is unreasonable for the purchaser to rely, on the skill and judgement of the supplier. For example, if a contractor is engaged by an employer to provide materials, such as components of a curtain walling system, against a performance specification, both implied terms will apply to the materials supplied since the intended purpose is known and the employer relies on the contractor's skill and judgement in selecting appropriate materials. Where a contractor is engaged to supply materials that are specified by the employer's consultant, only the implied term of satisfactory quality will apply. The contractor is not required to provide materials that are fit for purpose, since the employer relies on the consultant, not the contractor, to select what is required.

- A contract for the sale or supply of goods is, ordinarily, subject to similar implied terms concerning the satisfactory quality and fitness for purpose of the goods sold or supplied to those that apply to materials supplied under a contract for work and materials.
- A contract for construction work is, ordinarily, subject to an implied term that, where the purpose of the work is made known to the contractor, and the employer reasonably relies on the contractor's skill and judgement in deciding what should be constructed, the completed work will be reasonably fit for that purpose. But, as with materials supplied under such a contract, there will be no such obligation where the employer does not rely on the contractor's expertise, for instance because the contractor is engaged to construct work designed and specified by the employer's consultant.

The principal implied terms concerning property in what is sold or supplied are as follows.

- A contract for the sale of goods is, ordinarily, subject to an implied term that the seller has the right to sell the goods or will have the right to do so at the time when property is to pass to the buyer under the contract and that the goods are free, and will remain free until property is to pass, from any charge or encumbrance not disclosed to or known to the buyer before the contract is made.
- A contract for the work and materials is, ordinarily, subject to similar implied terms concerning property in the material supplied, as those in a contract of sale.

The principal implied terms concerning cooperation are as follows.

- A contract for construction works is, ordinarily, subject to an implied term that where the contractor's performance of its work requires the employer's cooperation, that cooperation will be forthcoming. This duty means, for example, that where the work cannot proceed unless the employer obtains the necessary consents, such as planning permissions, the employer will obtain those consents in sufficient time to enable the contractor to carry out the work without delay.
- A contract for construction works will, ordinarily, be subject to an implied term that neither party will prevent the other from performing the contract. But there is no implied warranty in a construction contract that the site is fit for the intended work.
- A contract for consultancy services is, ordinarily, subject to similar implied terms concerning cooperation and prevention of performance as those of a construction contract.
- If a construction contract provides for any entitlement under its terms to be certified by a contract administrator, such as an architect, it will, ordinarily, be subject to an implied term that the employer will make the necessary appointment and will not interfere with that person's certifying duties.

4.4 Exemption clauses

This publication is not concerned with specific terms that might be agreed in a contract concerning a construction project. For such information reference should be made to commentaries on the various standard form contracts published in the industry. There is, however, one type of term that needs particular consideration during the negotiations and conclusion of a contract if it is to be effective. This is the **exemption clause**.

4.4.1 Types of exemption clause

An exemption clause is a contract term by which one party, usually but not invariably the party proposing the terms of contract, seeks to avoid or exempt itself from what would otherwise be its obligations or liability under the contract (an **exclusion clause**), or seeks to restrict or limit its liability in some way (a **limitation clause**). An exemption clause can work indirectly by, for instance, restricting the enforcement of obligations under a contract, or by making enforcement unusually onerous.

Exemption clauses are commonly found in standard terms of business. For example, a seller of goods may seek to limit its obligations by providing in its standard terms that they form the whole agreement of the parties, and no terms are to be implied at law. The purpose of such wording is to exclude the implied terms of quality and title that would otherwise apply to the contract. A consultant may provide in its terms of appointment that any liability, whether for default under the contract or in negligence, is limited to a specific sum. The purpose of such a provision is to cap the consultant's potential liability to its client.

Because exemption clauses exclude or limit what would otherwise be a party's obligations or liabilities under a contract, they must be clearly incorporated and clearly worded if they are to be effective. There are also various statutory controls over the effectiveness of such provisions, and, in a few instances, criminal sanctions are imposed on those who seek to include such clauses in their contracts.

4.4.2 Incorporation and interpretation of exemption clauses

The successful incorporation of exemption clauses depends, to some extent, on how the parties conclude their contract.

- Where parties conclude a contract by signing a document setting out all of its terms they will, unless one is known by the other to be illiterate, be assumed to have read what they have signed. Thus the parties will be bound by the terms in that document, including any exemption clauses, even if they did not read the document. For example, if a client appoints a consultant by signing a copy of the consultant's standard terms, the client will be bound by those terms even if it has not read them.

- If a contract incorporates, by reference, terms in a document proposed by one of the parties, and that document contains unusually onerous terms, such as unusual exemption clauses, those terms may fail to be incorporated unless the party to whom the document is proposed knew that it was likely to contain such terms, for instance because both parties are businessmen operating in an industry where such terms are commonplace, or those terms, not just the document in which they can be found, are clearly drawn to that party's attention. For example, if a client appoints a consultant by signing the consultant's appointment letter, and that letter incorporates the consultant's standard terms by reference, the client may not be bound by exemption clauses contained in those standard terms unless, as might be the case with a developer, it is familiar with such terms, or its attention has been drawn to those clauses, for example in the appointment letter or at the meeting before the letter was signed.

Even if an exemption clause is successfully incorporated into a contract, it will be only effective if it clearly and unambiguously covers the circumstances that would otherwise give rise to liability. Exemption clauses are narrowly (strictly) interpreted (**construed**), with any uncertainty in meaning resolved against the party relying on the clause (the **contra proferentem rule**). Thus a clause in a consultant's appointment that limits the consultant's liability to its client for any claims under its appointment may not protect the consultant from claims brought by the client in the tort of negligence.

4.4.3 Statutory controls over exemption clauses

The main controls over exemption clauses that are relevant to those engaged in the construction industry are contained in the Unfair Contract Terms Act 1977 (the 1977 Act), and the Unfair Terms in Consumer Contracts Regulations 1999 (the 1999 Regulations). Both the 1977 Act and the 1999 Regulations are principally concerned with imposing controls over exemption clauses in consumer contracts for the benefit of consumers, but their ambit is different. The 1977 Act includes controls over exemption clauses in non-consumer contracts but is principally concerned with contracts for the sale or supply of goods, contracts for work and materials and contracts for services. The 1999 Regulations apply only to consumer contracts but cover a wider range of contract types than the 1977 Act, such as contracts for land, insurance contracts and arbitration agreements.

The 1977 Act and the 1999 Regulations do not use the same definitions of consumer and consumer contract.

- In general, a **consumer** is a party that neither contracts nor holds itself out as contracting for the purpose of a trade profession or business. A consumer must, under the 1999 Regulations, be an individual. Under the 1977 Act, any legal person can be a consumer.
- A **consumer contract** is a contract entered into between a consumer and a business, including but not limited to a contract for goods or services. A business is a party that contracts for the purpose of a trade, profession or business.

Thus all consultants, contractors and specialists engaged in the construction industry are businesses for the purpose of this legislation. But the client for whom they work may be a consumer. This will always be the case, both under the 1977 Act and the 1999 Regulations, where the client is an individual procuring work on their own home. It may also be the case where the client, although in business, is not procuring work for the purpose of that business provided, in the case of the 1999 Regulations, the client is an individual.

4.4.4 Exemption clauses that attract criminal sanctions

It is a criminal office for a business to include, in a consumer contract for the sale or supply of goods (including a contract for work and materials), a term that purports to exclude or restrict liability for breach of the terms concerning title and quality of goods and materials implied by statute into such contracts.
Thus a builder who contracts with a homeowner on terms that purport to restrict or exclude the builder's obligations to provide materials of satisfactory quality or that are fit for purpose, or purport to limit the builder's liability for breach of such obligations, is committing an offence. It is for this reason that the standard terms of builders and suppliers operating in the domestic market usually include statements to the effect that any such exemptions do not operate against consumers and do not affect statutory rights.

Criminal sanctions do not apply to those who exclude or restrict other contractual obligations or liabilities, such as liabilities for defects in services, or liabilities owned to persons other than consumers. Thus, in practice, the existence of criminal sanctions is of more concern to contractors, specialists and suppliers, particularly those who regularly deal with consumers, such as those who install replacement windows and doors, conservatories, and loft extensions, than to consultants.

4.4.5 Exemption clauses that are ineffective under the Unfair Contract Terms Act 1977

Certain types of exemption clause are rendered ineffective by the 1977 Act irrespective of the circumstances:

* any contract term or notice that purports to exempt or restrict a business from liability for death or personal injury resulting from negligence, including breach of a contractual duty of skill and care;
* any term in a consumer contract for the sale or supply of goods (including a contract for work and materials) that purports to

exclude or restrict liability for breach of the terms concerning title and quality of goods or materials implied by statute into such contracts.

4.4.6 Exemption clauses that may be ineffective under the Unfair Contract Terms Act 1977

Certain types of exemption clause are rendered ineffective by the 1977 Act unless they can be shown to be a fair and reasonable term to have included at the time that the contract was made having regard to the circumstances that were, or ought to have been, known at that time:

- any contract term that purports to exempt or restrict a business from liability (other than for death or personal injury) resulting from negligence, including breach of a contractual duty of skill and care;
- any term in a consumer contract that purports to exempt or restrict a business from liability for breach of contract;
- any term in a business's standard written terms that purports to exempt or restrict that business from liability, whether to a consumer or another business, for breach of contract;
- any term in a contract for the sale or supply of goods (including a contract for work and materials), other than a consumer contract, that purports to exclude or restrict liability for breach of the implied terms concerning title and quality of goods or materials implied by statute into such contracts.

In deciding whether an exemption clause is fair and reasonable, consideration is given to factors such as the relative strength of the parties' bargaining positions, whether the party against whom the term is imposed knew or ought reasonably to have known of that term, and whether it had an opportunity to conclude a similar contract without that term. Also relevant, in the case of limitation clauses, are the resources available to the party imposing that clause to meet the liability in question and whether the liability could have been insured.

In practice, this means that an exemption clause is more likely to be fair and reasonable if it is openly negotiated between the parties, some inducement is given to its inclusion in the contract (such as a reduction in price), and any limit on liability is proportionate to the resources and insurance cover of the person relying on that clause.

4.4.7 Exemption clauses that may be ineffective under the Unfair Terms in Consumer Contracts Regulations 1999

The 1999 Regulations invalidate any term of a consumer contract, other than one that defines, in clear words, the main subject of the contract or its price or that reflects mandatory statutory or regulatory provisions of law, that is not individually negotiated with the consumer and is unfair within the meaning of the Regulations.

- A term is not individually negotiated if it is drafted in advance and the consumer is not, therefore, able to influence its substance. An exemption clause included in a standard form consultancy agreement proposed by the consultant would fall into this category.
- A term is unfair if, contrary to the requirement of good faith, it causes a significant imbalance in the parties' rights and obligations arising under the contract, to the determent of the consumer.

The 1999 Regulations list a wide range of types of terms with which they are concerned and which, in appropriate circumstances, may be regarded as unfair. This list includes, in addition to the usual types of exemption clause, clauses that require the consumer to take disputes to arbitration rather than to court, that restrict the evidence available to the consumer, that impose penalties on the consumer or that entitle the supplier or seller to unilaterally vary its, or the consumer's, obligations under the contract.

A clause is not unfair merely because it is of a type listed in the 1999 Regulations. The requirement of good faith must also be contravened, this being concerned with matters similar to those that govern the test of reasonableness that applies under the Unfair

Contract Terms Act 1977. Thus an exemption clause is more likely to be effective if, as is the case under the 1977 Act, it is openly negotiated between the parties, some inducement is given to its inclusion in the contract (such as a reduction in price), and any limit on liability is proportionate to the resources and insurance cover of the person relying on that clause.

4.4.8 Exemption clauses in practice

The various controls over exemption clauses are of particular importance for consultants since they generally seek to contract on terms and conditions published by their professional bodies. Such terms almost invariably contain exemption clauses limiting the duration, amount or scope of the consultant's liability. They are wholly ineffective to the extent that they seek to exclude or limit the consultant's liability for death or personal injury due to the consultant's failure to exercise skill and care. Otherwise, they will be ineffective unless they satisfy the requirement of reasonableness in the 1977 Act, and, if the consultant is appointed by an individual consumer, the requirement of fairness under the 1999 Regulations. The requirement of reasonableness is, in most cases, the more important requirement since it will apply to all exemption clauses that form part of the consultant's standard terms of business, irrespective of whether or not it is contracting with an individual consumer.

The implication of these controls is that a consultant should draw its client's attention to the exemption and dispute resolution clauses in its standard terms before the appointment is made, and negotiate these, and the extent of any exemptions and limitations, with the client.

Although the same controls over exemption clauses apply to construction contracts as to professional services contracts, in practice the impact is less. Standard form construction contracts, unlike standard form professional services contracts, are often drafted by industry bodies, such as the Joint Contracts Tribunal, with input from all sectors of the industry. In consequence, they contain fewer exemption clauses. Furthermore, where the employer appoints advisers, the selection of contract terms is usually made by the employer's advisers, and those terms are then imposed on the contractor, the supplier. This is not a situation with which the statutory controls over exemption clauses are, principally, concerned.

Construction contracts upon which the controls over exemption clauses have most impact are those entered into by a client, generally without professional advice, on a builder's standard terms, or where supply contracts or subcontracts for work and materials are concluded on the supplier or subcontractor standard terms.

5. Invalid contracts

See this chapter for:

- **the difference between void and avoidable contracts;**
- **the effect of a void or avoidable contract;**
- **contracts void for illegality and mistake;**
- **contracts avoidable for misrepresentation;**
- **contracts avoidable for duress and undue influence.**

5.1 Void and avoidable contracts

An agreement made between parties having the necessary capacity and in accordance with the requirements for a valid contract may, nevertheless, be invalid as a contract if it is void or avoidable.

A **void contract** is one that does not create legal relationships between the parties at all. An **avoidable contract** is one that does create legal relationships between the parties but which can be set aside (**rescinded**) at the choice (the **election**) of one of the parties (the **innocent party**). If an avoidable contract is rescinded it is treated, for most purposes, as if it had not created legal relationships between the parties concerned. But, in contrast to a void contract, an avoidable contract that is not rescinded continues to govern the parties' legal relationship in the same way as any other contract.

5.2 Void contracts

The principal circumstances that make a contract void are **illegality, statute, public policy** and **mistake**. Such circumstances are, however, exceptional and it is unusual for a contract to be voided on any of these grounds.

5.2.1 Illegality

A contract may be illegal at the time it is made, or it may become illegal because of the manner in which it is subsequently performed.

- A contract that is illegal when it is made (**initial illegality**) is void and unenforceable by either party. A contract is illegal when it is made if it cannot be performed without committing a crime. For example, a contract to dispose of stolen goods is void for initial illegality, as is a contract that cannot be performed without committing a regulatory offence, such as a contract to dispose of builder's rubble at an unlicensed site.

- A contract is illegal in performance (**subsequent illegality**) if one or both parties intend to perform it in an illegal way or for some illegal purpose. For example, a contract to pay for building works in cash, or to pay an employee in cash, with the intention of one or both parties that the payments will not come to the attention of the Inland Revenue or Customs and Excise and thus need not be included in tax or VAT returns, will be illegal. If both parties intend the contract to be performed in an illegal way, then neither can enforce it. If the illegal purpose is intended by one party but the other party is unaware of it, the latter can enforce the contract, but not the former. For example, if both parties to a contract for the demolition of a listed building intend that work to be done without obtaining the necessary consents, the contract will be void. If the contractor did not know that this was the client's intention, it can enforce the contract, but the employer cannot.

5.2.2 Statute and public policy

A contract may be void by **statute**. For example, wagering (gaming) contracts are voided by the Gaming Acts.

A contract may be unenforceable in whole or in part because of **public policy**. Thus a contract or term of a contract that restricts the freedom of one of the parties to carry on a trade or business with others may be unenforceable unless the restriction is reasonable having regard to the interests of the parties and the public.

- A provision in a contract of employment that the employee should not practise their profession for a period after leaving the employment is likely to be unenforceable as it prevents the employee earning a living by their profession.

- A provision that states that the employee should not provide services to their employer's clients for a period after leaving the employment and should not work for others during the period of their employment is likely to be upheld as reasonable, provided that the period of the restriction after the employment ceases is reasonable.

5.2.3 Mistake

A contract may, in exceptional circumstances, be void for **mistake**. There are a number of different possibilities.

- Where both parties are mistaken about the existence of the subject matter of the contract, the contract may be void for mistake. For example, a contract for the sale of a specific article such as a painting is void where, at the time of the contract, the painting has, unknown to either party, been destroyed.
- Where the parties are at cross-purposes about the subject matter of the contract, the contract may be void for mistake. Thus a contract for the purchase of specific goods currently on board a named ship is void if there are two ships of that name carrying such goods owned by the seller, and it cannot be established which cargo the contract is for.
- A more controversial situation is where one party is mistaken about the terms of the contract and the other party is aware of the mistake. Thus, if one person puts forward an offer and the person to whom the offer is addressed accepts it, knowing that the offer was not intended to be made on those terms, the resulting contract may be void. Similarly, an offer made to a named person cannot be accepted by someone else so as to create an enforceable contract. For example, an offer made to a company to provide goods or services cannot be accepted, on their own behalf, by one of the company's employees.
- Equally controversial is the situation where a party is mistaken about the identity of the person with whom they are dealing. Provided that the contract is concluded in person, such as in a shop purchase, not by exchange of letters, and the identity of the person, not merely their credit worthiness, is of fundamental

importance, the contract may be void.

A contract will not be void for mistake merely because one party is mistaken about the nature of its subject matter, or the value or commercial use of what is to be supplied, even if the other party is aware of this mistake. If, for example, a person purchases an unnamed painting in the belief that it is by a well-known master, the contract is not void merely because the painting is not by that person. It makes no difference whether or not the mistaken belief was known to the seller unless the mistake was induced by the seller, in which case the contract may be voidable for misrepresentation.

5.2.4 Void contracts in practice

The type of void contract most commonly encountered in the construction industry is one that is void for illegality because the parties agree to a discount for cash with a view to defrauding the Inland Revenue or HM Customs and Excise.

Such contracts are most prevalent where consultants or builders are engaged for the refurbishment of domestic property, the usual arrangement being that a reduced fee or price will be given for cash. Since the only reason that such a discount is offered is because cash payments will not show up in the supplier's books, and will not be subject to VAT or tax, the resulting contract will be void. The supplier will not be able to enforce a right to payment, and there is no contractual basis for seeking compensation from the supplier if the work provided is defective.

5.3 Avoidable contracts

The principal circumstances that make a contract avoidable are **misrepresentation, duress** and **undue influence**.

5.3.1 Misrepresentation

If a person (the **innocent party**) is induced to contract with another as a result of a false statement (a **misrepresentation**) made by the latter (the **representor**), the contract may be avoidable for **misrepresentation**.

The statement must be a statement of fact made by the representor, or on its behalf, to the innocent party with the intention or expectation that the statement will come to the innocent party's attention.

- The statement can be express or implied. For example, an express statement that a house does not have dry rot may contain an implied statement that it has been inspected for dry rot.
- A statement of opinion or belief will be regarded as a statement of fact if it is made in circumstances where it can be assumed that the maker of that statement has reasonable grounds for that opinion or belief. A statement by a house-owner that the local authority would be likely to give planning approval for a roof extension might not be regarded as a statement of fact since there would be no basis for implying that a private individual had reasonable grounds for such a belief. If, however, the house owner was an architect it might well be regarded as a statement of fact since an architect could be assumed to have reasonable grounds for expressing such an opinion.
- A statement of intention is not a statement of fact except to the extent that it implies that the maker of the statement has the stated intention at the time it makes the statement.

The statement must induce the contract. The statement need not be the sole inducement but it must have influenced the person to whom it was made to conclude a contract with the maker of the statement.

- There is no inducement if, at the time the contract is made, the innocent party is not aware that the statement has been made.
- There is no inducement if the innocent party knew that the statement was false or would have entered into the contract even if they had known that the statement was false. For example, if a developer is proposing to demolish and rebuild a property, it may be difficult for it to show that it was induced to purchase that property on the basis of a statement that it was free of dry rot.
- There is no inducement if the innocent party relies on their own advisers in respect of matters referred to in statement, not

the statement itself. If, for example, a purchaser of a business has the accounts examined by its own advisers, it will be difficult for it to establish that it was induced to purchase the business because of representations about turnover and profit made by the vendor.

- There can be inducement even if the innocent party could have discovered, or was provided with the means of discovering, that the statement was false but did not do so. For instance, a purchaser of a business is not prevented from contending that it did so on the basis of false statements about turnover and profit made by the vendor, merely because it was provided with the accounts, which, had it looked at them, would have shown the true position.

A statement is a misrepresentation if it is untrue when it is made or, despite being true when made, it becomes untrue before the contract is concluded.

- A statement is a misrepresentation if the maker knows it is false or, without knowing it is false, shuts their eyes to the possibility that it might be false.
- A statement may be a misrepresentation even if it is made innocently, that is without knowing it to be false or where the maker shuts their eyes to the possibility that it might be false. For example, if a package tour company represents in its brochure that a hotel is in a quiet situation, that statement will be false if, at the time it is made or later, before the holiday is booked, a discotheque opens up next door, even if the tour operator had no reason to know this.
- The maker of a statement that is true when made is, up until a contract is made, under a continuing obligation to correct that statement if it becomes false or, in the case of a statement of opinion or belief, they subsequently learn that the statement is or has become false.
- Since, in general, a person has no duty to disclose information to someone with whom they are negotiating in a commercial context, a failure to disclose information that is relevant to a proposed contract, however dishonest that failure might seem,

is not, in itself, a misrepresentation. Acquiescence in another's self-deception is not a misrepresentation unless the deception results from one's own statements or half-truths. Thus an antique dealer who is aware that a purchaser is offering too much for a piece of furniture because they think the piece is a Chippendale, when it is a reproduction, is not obliged to reveal the truth, unless the dealer induced that belief in the purchaser.

- There are a few instances where contract parties are required to deal with each other on the basis of utmost good faith (*uberrimae fides*). The most commonly encountered example concerns contracts of insurance. The person purchasing the policy must make full disclosure of all facts that are material to the proposed contract. If this is not done, the contract may be avoidable at the option of the insurer.

If a contract is avoidable for misrepresentation the innocent party can **rescind** it by notice to the other party provided that the parties can, possibly with some financial recompense, be returned to more or less the positions they were in prior to the contract being concluded. But this will be possible only if the recession does not affect the rights of others and the contract is not affirmed by the party to whom the representation was made after discovering that it was false.

- Contracts for the purchase of property, such as a vehicle or a house, can, unless the property has been sold on to a third person, generally be rescinded for misrepresentation. The purchase price can be returned in exchange for the property and a financial adjustment made between the parties to allow for any deterioration or improvement in the property after it was purchased.
- It is usually not possible to rescind a contract that involves the supply of services, such as a consultant's appointment, or the supply of work and materials, such as a building contract, once performance has commenced. This is because it is not possible to return what has been performed.
- A contract is affirmed if, once the misrepresentation comes to

light, the innocent party continues to accept the validity of the contract, for example by making payments under it, such as rent under a lease, or by insisting on performance by the other, for instance by requesting further deliveries of goods. Failure to rescind a contract for a long period, years rather than months, may, in itself, be regarded as affirmation.

5.3.2 Damages for negligence and fraud

If a misrepresentation is made **negligently** or **fraudulently**, the innocent party may be entitled to compensation for any losses suffered by entering into the contract, irrespective of whether or not the contract can be, or is, rescinded.

- If a contractor suffers loss by entering into a contract on the basis of incorrect information contained, for instance, in plans, specifications or ground investigation reports included in the tender documents, it may be entitled to compensation from the employer for negligent misrepresentation unless the client can show that it believed in and had reasonable grounds to believe in the correctness of that information up to the date of the contract.
- If a business is purchased on the basis of misrepresentations by the vendor which the vendor knew were false or made recklessly, not caring whether they were true or false, the purchaser will be entitled to damages in fraud compensating them for all the loses incurred by purchasing the business.

5.3.3 Duress

If a person (the innocent party) enters into a contract because of wrongful pressure exerted by the other party to that contract, the contract may be avoidable for **duress** provided that the effect of the pressure is that the innocent party has no practical alternative but to submit by entering into the contract. For a contract to be avoidable for duress, the wrongful pressure must be of the following types.

- Unlawful threats of physical violence or of imprisonment made to the innocent party, their family or, possibly, others. For example, if a householder agrees to pay for building works carried out on their home because of physical threats by the builder, the householder may be able to rescind that contract for duress.

- Unlawful threats of or damage to the victim's property or of unlawful detention of the victim's property. For example, if a developer contracts to pay a subcontractor directly for work carried out by the subcontractor under its subcontract with a now insolvent builder, because the subcontractor threatens to destroy or remove its work if those payments are not made, the developer may be entitled to rescind that contract for duress.
- Unlawful threats to damage the victim's economic interests by committing a tort or crime or, provided that bad faith or similar can be shown, by not honouring or repudiating an existing contract with the innocent party. For example, if a consultant agrees, by variation of its existing appointment, to accept a reduced fee from a client because the client, not believing that it has grounds to do so, threatens that it will otherwise repudiate the existing appointment or become insolvent, the consultant may be entitled to rescind the variation agreement for economic duress. If the client's statements about the consequence of the consultant not agreeing a reduced fee reflect commercial realities, they do not amount to economic duress.

A contract is avoidable for duress only if the wrongful pressure is of sufficient gravity to mean that the innocent party had little alternative but to accede to that pressure instead of, for instance, pursuing other remedies through the courts. The wrongful pressure must also be a sufficient cause of the innocent party's decision to conclude the contract. In the case of threats of physical violence, it is sufficient that the exerted pressure is one of the reasons, not necessarily the only reason, why the contract is concluded. In the case of threats to property or economic interests the pressure exerted must, given the circumstances at the time, be a significant cause of or, possibly, coercive of the innocent party's decision to enter into the contract. Something more than normal commercial pressure is necessary.

If a contract is avoidable for duress, it can be rescinded by the innocent party provided that this is done promptly once they are no longer affected by the wrongful pressure. If the contract is not rescinded promptly, the innocent party may be considered to have been affirmed and the right to rescind will be lost.

5.3.4 Undue influence

A contract may be avoidable for **undue influence** where actual undue influence is shown or where undue influence is assumed.

- A contract is avoidable for **actual undue influence** where one party, or its agent, exercises such a degree of domination or control over the other (the innocent party) that the innocent party's ability to make an independent decision about whether or not to enter into the contract is substantially undermined. For instance, if a religious adviser uses their spiritual influence to obtain pecuniary advantage from members of their flock, the contracts giving effect to that pecuniary advantage may be avoidable.
- A contract is avoidable for **assumed undue influence** if the relationship between the parties, or between a party's agent and the victim, is of a type in which such influence is assumed and the contract entered into by the parties is to the manifest disadvantage of the innocent party, thus suggesting that the influence has been abused. Relationships in which undue influence is assumed are those in which one party will necessarily have the confidence of the other and the influence over the other that naturally grows out of this confidence. Examples include parent and child, solicitor and client, and husband and wife. Commercial relationships, such as between architect and householder, developer and builder, or contractor and specialist do not give rise to a presumption of undue influence.
- A contract entered into because of undue influence exercised by a third person on the innocent party may be avoidable if the other party to the contract had actual or constructive knowledge that undue influence was being exerted. Constructive knowledge means, in this respect, knowledge that the relationship between the innocent party and the third person is one in which undue influence can be assumed and that the contract does not appear to be to the advantage of the innocent party. For example,

if a wife, at her husband's request, gives a bank a charge over the
matrimonial home to secure the husband's debts, the charge may
be avoidable by the wife if the bank is aware of the relationship
and the charge is to the wife's disadvantage.
• Where a relationship between the innocent party and the other
party to the contract, or a third person, is one in which undue
influence is assumed, the presumption can be rebutted by showing
that the innocent party acted on competent independent advice
or entered into the contract despite receiving independent advice
that they should not do so. Thus, in the above example, the bank
can minimise the risk of the charge on the matrimonial home
being avoided by ensuring that the wife takes proper independent
advice before granting the charge in its favour.

A contract that is avoidable for undue influence can be rescinded
at the option of the innocent party, if they have not affirmed the
contract after the undue influence ends. But this will only be
possible if the parties can, with financial recompense if necessary,
be returned, more or less, to the positions that they were in prior
to the contract being concluded, without affecting the rights of
other persons who cannot be compensated in money.

5.3.5 Avoidable contracts in practice

In the construction industry, the most commonly encountered
situation where a contract is likely to be avoidable is where it has
been induced by misrepresentation. This is because, during
negotiations, there is always a temptation to encourage a deal by
selling it to the other party. It is important that such salesmanship
does not stray into the area of misrepresentation.

Another situation in which a contract may be avoidable for
misrepresentation is where one party is dependent principally on
information provided by the other in deciding the price at which it
is proposed to contract. For instance, where a builder is asked to
tender on the basis of information provided by the employer or its
advisers, the builder may be able to argue that it was induced to
contract on the basis of that information and, since the information

is erroneous, it is entitled to avoid the contract for misrepresentation if work has not started, or, if it has, recover compensation for negligent misrepresentation.

Such claims are relatively rare because most standard form building contracts, such as those published by the Joint Contracts Tribunal, allocate the risks of errors in the tender information to the employer. If the contract places the risk of such errors on the contractor, it is usual to find provisions by which the contractor acknowledges that it has carried out its own investigations into such matters and has not relied on the tender information, the intention being to preclude claims in misrepresentation where the information is inaccurate. Such provisions, covering site and geological information provided by the employer, are common in standard form engineering contracts. A similar intention underlies provisions in design and build contracts that state that the contractor accepts responsibility for the accuracy of the employer's requirements included in the tender documents.

Contracts that are avoidable for duress or undue influence are rarely encountered in the construction industry. But where threats are used to persuade a party to renegotiate the terms of an existing contract, there is a possibility that the pressure, if more than merely commercial pressure, will provide grounds for avoiding the renegotiated terms on the grounds of economic duress.

6. Letters of intent

See this chapter for:

- **the nature and purpose of a letter of intent;**
- **when to issue a letter of intent;**
- **the legal effect of a letter of intent;**
- **how to prepare a letter of intent.**

6.1 Use of letters of intent

Contract negotiations often extend over a considerable period, since questions of price, scope of work and terms must all be agreed and, if prices are obtained by tender, price reductions may have to be considered, before a contract can be concluded. Time for concluding such negotiations may be a luxury that the party procuring work does not have. A developer may be working to a programme that requires a consultant to commence design work or a preferred contractor to commence construction immediately, even though uncertainties about the scope of work and price are unresolved. A client may be a public body whose administrative procedures are such that contract documents cannot be prepared for signature until many months after the successful tenderer is selected and work is programmed to start. Delivery periods for specified components or materials may be such that, if the envisaged completion date is to be achieved, they must be ordered before the construction contract is let. A contractor may be under pressure, once its tender is accepted, to instruct the preferred subcontractors to commence work immediately, before terms and prices can be finalised, so that the contract completion date can be achieved.

In all such cases there is a conflict between the demand for work to commence immediately and the need for further time to conclude the anticipated contract for that work. Such conflicts are common in the construction industry. The usual solution is to issue a **letter of intent**. This is a letter written by or on behalf of the person wishing to procure work to the intended supplier of that work, recording the intention to contract for that work once the outstanding matters are resolved and asking the supplier to commence the work, or a certain part of the work, in the meantime.

If the parties eventually conclude the envisaged contract, then the letter of intent is of no further significance since the work carried out under its terms will be governed by the parties' contract. But in some cases the envisaged contract is never concluded. This may be because the parties are unable to agree terms or, even if terms are eventually agreed, one of the parties, usually the supplier, is unwilling to sign up to those terms, because of changed circumstances. For example, the supplier may be concerned that its performance is falling short of what is required of it under the proposed contract.

In such cases, it is important to know whether the letter of intent is of any legal effect.

6.2 The legal effect of a letter of intent

The legal effect of a letter of intent depends on the words used in the letter, interpreted in the light of the circumstances at the time it is issued and acted on. There are three possibilities. The letter may be of no binding effect, it may give rise to a **unilateral contract** (an 'if' contract, as it is sometimes called), or it may result in a **bilateral contract**.

6.2.1 No binding effect

A letter of intent has no binding effect if it fails to create contractual obligations. If this is the case, the supplier is not obliged to comply with the request or, having started, to continue with the work. The person requesting the work is not contractually obliged to pay for it, but will, if the request is made in a commercial context and the letter of intent does not provide otherwise, have to pay, under the law of restitution, a reasonable sum (a *quantum meruit*) for what is provided.

• The assessment of a reasonable sum is not governed by the terms of contract that are envisaged when the letter of intent is written, although if the supplier has provided prices for the work these may be relevant.

- A reasonable sum may be a greater or a lesser sum than the amount that would have been payable had the intended contract been concluded. For example, a reasonable sum payable for work provided, at request, by a design and build contractor could include separate amounts for its actual design and its construction costs, even if, under the anticipated contract, the design costs were to be absorbed in a lump sum price for the construction work.
- A reasonable sum may include not only the actual cost of providing the requested work but also a reasonable allowance for the supplier's profits and overheads.
- A reasonable sum should reflect the quality of the work provided. Less will be payable for defective work than for work that is properly executed. But costs incurred by the person requesting the work because of the manner in which it is provided are not, ordinarily, relevant in assessing a reasonable sum. For example, costs incurred because of delays by the supplier are not relevant in assessing a reasonable sum for the work supplied.
- Because there is no mutuality of obligations, there will, ordinarily, be no legal basis for claims by the person requesting the work against the supplier. For example, there is no basis for claims against the supplier for losses, such as losses caused by delay or disruption, incurred by the party requesting the work because of the manner in which it was carried out.

A letter of intent is unlikely to be of binding effect if, at the time it is written, the principal terms of the anticipated contract between the parties, such as those concerning payment and scope of work, have yet to be agreed. Uncertainty about such matters prevents a contract coming into existence by conduct when the requested work is provided.

Even if the principal terms of the envisaged contract are resolved when the letter of intent is written, the wording of the letter itself and the circumstances at the time may show that the parties did not intend to be contractually bound until a written contract was prepared and signed by them. This may be expressly stated in the letter of intent, or may be implicit from the words of the letter considered in context. For example, a letter of intent may use the formula often found in correspondence concerning the purchase of land 'subject to contract'. The letter may state that the parties are unable to contract until formal contract documents are drawn up and signed, and the context may indicate that the preparation and signing of such documents is not merely intended to be an administrative step to record a previously agreed contract, but is to be a pre-condition to any contract between the parties.

6.2.2 A unilateral contract

A letter of intent may amount to a **unilateral contract** (an 'if' contract). A unilateral contract is one that imposes obligations on only one of the parties – in the case of a letter of intent, the party requesting the work.

The supplier is not obliged to comply with the request and, having commenced work, is not under any obligation to continue with or complete it. The party requesting the work is, however, contractually obliged to pay for work supplied in accordance with the terms of the letter of intent, and may not withdraw its request for that work once the other party starts to perform. A good example of a unilateral contract is an offer of a reward for the return of lost property. No one is obliged to find the property concerned, but if it is returned, the reward must be paid.

- There is some uncertainty over whether a unilateral contract comes into existence when the requested performance commences, or when it is completed. In the case of work requested by letter of intent, the contract probably comes into existence when the party requested to provide the work starts to do so, otherwise the promise to pay could be withdrawn before the work was completed. If this analysis is correct, then a letter of intent may give rise to a construction contract and be subject to the provisions concerning payment and dispute resolution in the Housing Grants, Construction and Regeneration Act 1996, Part II.

- Under a unilateral contract the obligation to pay is conditional upon performance of the work in the requested manner, so there is greater scope for stipulating what payment is to be made and how the work is to be performed than is the case where a letter of intent is of no binding effect. It is possible, for example, to stipulate that payments will depend not only on the work complying with the relevant specifications but also on the work being carried out in accordance with other requirements, such as programme; but care should be taken to ensure that the mechanism for payment complies with the requirements in the Housing Grants, Construction and Regeneration Act 1996, Part II, if applicable.
- A letter of intent that takes effect as a unilateral contract is, in one respect, similar to a letter of intent in that it is of no binding effect. Because it does not impose obligations on the supplier, there is, ordinarily, no legal basis for claims against the supplier by the person requesting the work.

A letter of intent is likely to be interpreted as a unilateral contract where it contains detailed provisions governing the circumstances in which payment will be made to the person providing the work and when unless the wording of the letter, or the surrounding circumstances, show that a bilateral contract came into existence, or that the parties did not intend to contract on the terms of that letter.

6.2.3 A bilateral contract

A letter of intent may give rise to a **bilateral contract**, formed by conduct, when the supplier of the requested work starts to provide that work. If a bilateral contract is concluded, each party has obligations to the other.

- If a bilateral contract is formed when the offer contained in a letter of intent is accepted by conduct, it will be no different from any other bilateral contract. Both parties will be bound by the terms of, or incorporated into, the letter.
- Because a bilateral contract gives rise to mutual obligations, the supplier will be contractually obliged to perform the work in

accordance with the terms of the letter of intent. If it fails to do so, it may be liable to the other party for losses incurred as a result of that failure. The person requesting the work will, in turn, be obliged to pay for the work in accordance with the terms of the letter of intent.

- A bilateral contract formed on the basis of a letter of intent may be a construction contract subject to the provisions concerning payment and dispute resolution in the Housing Grants, Construction and Regeneration Act 1996, Part II.

A letter of intent is likely to have effect as a bilateral contract where its terms impose obligations on both parties, those terms are sufficiently certain to have contractual effect, and neither the wording of the letter nor the circumstances at the time show that the parties did not intend to contract on those terms: for instance because fundamental aspects of the parties' relationship, such as price and scope of works, have yet to be negotiated or the letter makes clear that the parties do not intend to contract until a formal contract is drawn up and executed.

6.3 Preparing a letter of intent

The wording of a letter of intent should reflect the legal effect it is intended to have. This should be considered in the light of factors such as why the anticipated contract for the work cannot be concluded at the time, why it is necessary for work to commence before that contract can be concluded, or how much work is to be instructed before a contract is concluded.

6.3.1 Preparing a letter of intent to create a bilateral contract

If all the terms of the anticipated contract are agreed but, for internal administrative reasons, contract documents are not ready for signature, it may be appropriate to issue a letter of intent in the form of an offer of a contract on the terms already agreed, pending the execution of contract documents once prepared. The letter of intent should identify the agreed terms, for instance by reference to the tender documents and the contractor's tender, and provide that the parties will execute formal documents embodying these terms, when available. In effect, the obligation to execute a formal contract becomes a term of the offer set out in the letter of intent. A bilateral contract on those terms will come into existence when work starts. The subsequent execution of contract documents is merely an administrative procedure formally recording the previously agreed terms.

A letter of intent concerning only part of the work to be provided under the anticipated contract, for instance long delivery items, may also be prepared to take effect as a bilateral contract to provide and pay for that work. But, particularly if the person being asked to provide that work is not the preferred main contractor but a supplier of the long delivery items, it may be preferable to prepare and agree a separate contract for that work, identifying matters such as specification, programme, delivery and payment and what is to happen if the main contract works are postponed or cancelled.

6.3.2 Preparing a letter of intent to create a unilateral contract

If the terms of the anticipated contract have yet to be agreed, or one or other party is not prepared to enter into a contract before all of the necessary documents are prepared and executed, a letter of intent taking effect as a bilateral contract is not appropriate. The letter of intent should be written either to take effect as a unilateral contract or to be of no binding effect.

From the perspective of the person requesting the work, it may be preferable for the letter of intent to be written to take effect as a unilateral contract. This is likely to give greater control over the circumstances in which payment must be made than a letter of intent that is of no binding effect. On the other hand, if a letter of intent takes effect as a unilateral contract when work commences, it will, ordinarily, be subject to the provisions for payment and dispute resolution in the Housing Grants, Construction and Regeneration Act 1996. The Act's requirement to make interim payments for the work supplied may not be acceptable to the party requesting that work.

If a letter of intent is intended to give rise to a unilateral contract, the following matters should be considered in preparing the letter.

- The letter should identify, even if only in general terms, the matters that have to be resolved before the anticipated contract can be concluded. It should make clear that until these matters are resolved the only obligations between the parties will be the obligation of the party on whose behalf the letter is written to pay for work that is supplied in accordance with the terms of the letter of intent, in particular the specification and programme for the work set out or referred to in the letter.
- Although this may be implied, the letter should state that, once the anticipated contract is concluded, that contract will supersede the letter of intent and apply retrospectively to all work provided under that letter.
- The letter should identify the work being requested pending the conclusion of the anticipated contract and the documents, such as specifications and drawings, that govern how the work is to be carried out. If the work has been tendered for, reference can be made to the specifications and drawings included in the invitation to tender. General references to the terms on which the anticipated contract is to be concluded should be avoided since, if these are incorporated, the letter of intent may take effect as a bilateral, not a unilateral, contract.
- The letter should identify the basis for and timing of payment for the requested work. It should indicate how non-compliance with the requirements for the work, such as programme, will affect payment, and how payment will be assessed if the envisaged contract is not concluded or the work is abandoned. Since the letter of intent is to take effect as a unilateral contract, the payment provisions should comply with the requirements of the Housing Grants, Construction and Regeneration Act 1996, Part II. In order to avoid the complexities of devising a payment regime specifically for work supplied under the letter of intent, it may be appropriate to state that, pending the conclusion of the anticipated contract, payment for the requested work will be made in accordance with the interim payment provisions in the standard

terms on which the envisaged contract will be concluded, if these are known at the time. But care should be taken to ensure that those provisions sufficiently link payment to the manner in which the work is provided, for instance compliance with programme, not merely to the quality of what is provided. If this is not the case, the person requesting the work may have no recourse if they suffer loss because of the manner in which the work is provided.

- The provision of work under a letter of intent, even one that takes effect as a unilateral contract, may be or become more advantageous to the supplier than its provision under the anticipated contract, for instance because the manner or timing of the supply does not accord with the terms of the anticipated contract. In order to overcome any reluctance that the supplier might have to enter into the envisaged contract, the right to payment under a letter of intent is sometimes linked to the anticipated contract being concluded within a stated period of time or to the party providing the requested work not obstructing the conclusion of the anticipated contract. Such provisions are difficult to draft effectively, and may conflict with the payment regime required by the Housing Grants, Construction and Regeneration Act 1996, Part II. They may also make it more likely that the requested work will be abandoned if the anticipated contract is not concluded. This may not be an acceptable risk to the party requesting the work.

6.3.3 Preparing a letter of intent that is to have no binding effect

If a letter of intent is not intended to have binding effect, the following matters should be considered.

- The letter should identify, even if only in general terms, the matters that have to be resolved before the envisaged contract can be concluded, and should make clear that until these matters are resolved there is to be no contract between the parties.
- Although this may be implied, the letter should state that, when the anticipated contract is concluded, that contract will supersede the letter of intent and apply retrospectively to all work provided under that letter.

- The letter should identify the work being requested pending the conclusion of the anticipated contract and documents, such as specifications and drawings, which govern how that work is to be carried out.
- If it is intended that the person providing the requested work should have a restitutionary right to a reasonable sum for what it provides, the letter need do no more than acknowledge that there is such an entitlement. If the restitutionary right to payment is to be qualified in any way, for instance by providing that payment will be conditional on compliance with programme dates, the letter of intent should be prepared to take effect as a unilateral contract.

6.4 Letters of intent in practice

If work is carried out under a letter of intent, there is greater uncertainty about the parties' rights and obligations than will be the case if the contract is concluded before work starts. It should not be assumed that these uncertainties can be ignored because the letter of intent will soon be superseded by the anticipated contract. Once work starts much of the impetus to overcoming difficulties about the terms of the anticipated contract will be lost. With each day that passes without the anticipated contract being concluded, there is an increased risk that the supplier of the work will not be prepared to agree terms because of concerns that, by doing so, it will be fixed with liability for inadequacies in the work supplied or in the manner of performance. This will be particularly so if the work falls behind the envisaged programme.

The decision to issue a letter of intent should, in consequence, not be taken lightly but only after a full review of matters such as the following.

- Need a letter of intent be issued at all? Why is it not possible to conclude a contract for the works in question in the normal way?
- Why is it necessary to start work before the anticipated contract is concluded? If a letter of intent is necessary, need it encompass all the work to be carried out under the envisaged contract? What is the minimum amount of work that must start immediately?

- How realistic is it to expect that the difficulties standing in the way of the anticipated contract will be overcome? If these difficulties are serious, would it not be better to postpone the start of work until they are overcome?
- If work does commence immediately, will this adversely affect the prospects of concluding the anticipated contract?
- What legal effect is the proposed letter of intent to have? Should the wording of the letter be discussed with the recipient before it is issued?
- What will happen if the anticipated contract cannot be agreed or if the work to be carried out under that contract is postponed or abandoned?

Once a letter of intent is issued, progress towards concluding the anticipated contract should not be allowed to slip. Difficulties affecting the negotiations should be quickly identified and addressed. If these difficulties cannot be overcome, conscious decisions should be taken about whether the work being supplied under the letter of intent is to continue and on what terms.

If the letter of intent does not encompass all of the work to be provided under the anticipated contract – if for instance it is limited to long delivery items or to mobilisation or foundation work – work should not be allowed to progress beyond what was authorised by that letter without the anticipated contract being concluded or a further letter of intent being issued. If unauthorised work is provided it may be regarded as being supplied not under the terms of the letter of intent but under an implied request to the supplier to continue working. Although this implied request will entitle the supplier to payment on a restitutionary basis, there will be no mutuality of obligations as regards that work, and there may be great uncertainty about the standards to which the supplier is required to work.

7. Contracting procedures in the construction industry

See this chapter for:

- **negotiating and tendering for contracts;**
- **single-stage and two-stage tendering;**
- **statutory restrictions on procurement;**
- **contract procedures for employer-designated subcontractors;**
- **contracting and subcontracting for consultants' services;**
- **contracting and subcontracting for construction work;**
- **executing bonds and warranties.**

7.1 Identifying a preferred supplier and agreeing terms

The principal procedures used in the construction industry for agreeing contract terms are direct negotiation with a preferred supplier, invitation of competitive tenders from a number of possible suppliers on predetermined terms, or a combination of these approaches, such as direct negotiation with a preferred supplier identified though a tendering process.

7.2 Negotiated contracts

In a negotiated procedure the person requiring the work identifies a preferred supplier for that work and negotiates the terms of a contract directly with them. At the outset of the negotiations neither party may have a clear idea about the terms on which the contract is to be concluded or about the principal obligations to be undertaken, such as price and scope of work. If so, these matters need to be resolved during the negotiations. Alternatively the contract terms and scope of works may have already been decided by the person requiring the work. If so, the negotiations will principally concern matters such as price and programme.

In either case there is little element of competition, other than that which exists because the person requiring the work can look elsewhere if terms, such as those concerning price, scope and quality of work, cannot be agreed.

The negotiated procedure is frequently used to engage a consultant. This is because the selection of a consultant on the basis of reputation and quality of design work may be considered more important than selection on the basis of price. Furthermore, many consultants charge similar levels of fees for similar services and, even if there are differences, the potential savings are small compared with the overall cost of the project.

7.2.1 Selecting a preferred supplier with whom to negotiate

A preferred supplier is often identified informally on the basis of previous experience, personal recommendation or reputation. An element of competition or, more properly, comparison can be introduced into the negotiated procedure by interviewing a number of possible suppliers and, having considered their presentations about matters such as cost, quality of work and experience, selecting one with which to negotiate.

Where it is important to achieve a high quality design solution, a preferred supplier may be identified by an open or restricted design competition, with a view to negotiating a contract with the successful entrant. If a competition is proposed, matters such as the following should be considered and covered by the competition documents.

- Is the competition to be open to all or restricted to invited entrants?
- What amount of work can be expected of entrants?
- Are entrants to be remunerated, other than by prizes, for the work they provide?
- What copyright arrangements apply to submitted schemes?

If the competition entries are to be judged by independent assessors, it may be necessary to reserve the right not to engage the winning entrant, or any entrant to supply the work.

7.3 Tendered contracts

In a tender procedure, the person requiring work invites offers for it on the basis of tender documents prepared by them, or on their behalf. The tender documents should contain sufficient information about the work and the terms on which it is to be contracted to enable those preparing tenders to identify, assess and price the requirements and risks of the work. The tender documents should identify the information that is to be provided by tenderers when submitting their bids so that all tenders are presented in a similar format and are readily comparable with each other. It is preferable to identify the criteria against which tenders will be assessed in the tender documents, even if a right not to accept any of the submitted tenders is reserved.

7.3.1 Open invitation and restricted invitation

Tenders can be invited by open invitation or restricted invitation. Restricted invitation tendering is commonly used to procure construction work.

- **Open invitation tendering** involves publicising the intention to seek offers for the required work and sending tender documents to anyone who requests them. Tenders received by the specified date are assessed against threshold criteria such as technical capacity and financial standing, and a shortlist is identified. The shortlisted tenders are then assessed against the stated criteria for selection, such as price, and a preferred tenderer is identified, with which a contract for the work is concluded.
- **Restricted invitation tendering** involves selecting, by reference to criteria such as reputation, financial standing and willingness to tender, a limited number of persons from whom tenders are invited. Tender documents are issued to these persons, and tenders received by the specified date are assessed against the criteria for selection and a preferred tenderer is identified, with whom a contract for the work is concluded. The number of tenders is generally limited to about six, sometimes fewer where the preparation of tenders will, as in the case of a tender for design and build work, involve a significant input of time and expense.

...age tendering and two-stage tendering

commonly encountered tendering procedures in the
.uction industry are single-stage tendering and two-stage
.idering.

- In **single-stage tendering**, tenders are invited for the work in
  the form of offers that are capable of immediate acceptance.
  The tender documents should identify the terms of contract on
  which the tenderer, if successful, will be engaged and give sufficient
  information about the work so that it can be priced in the manner
  required by the tender documents, or the tenderers' proposals for
  the work can be completed in sufficient detail for a price to be
  given. For example, if tenders are invited for work described by
  performance specification, tenderers must be advised not only of
  the terms on which they will have to contract, if successful, but
  also whether they must include, with their price for the work,
  design proposals showing how they intend to meet the
  performance specification.
- In **two-stage tendering**, the objective is not to obtain offers for
  the work that can be immediately accepted, but to obtain initial
  (first-stage) tenders from which a preferred suppler is identified.
  Under this first stage, tenderers are required to provide, on the
  basis of the information included in the tender documents, a
  pricing structure that will, if they are successful at the first
  stage, form the basis of the second stage tender. Once a preferred
  supplier is identified, they develop employer's requirements for
  the work in consultation with the employer and its advisers to a
  stage where a final (second-stage) tender can be submitted based
  on the developed scheme and the pricing structure in its first-
  stage tender. If the second-stage tender is accepted, this forms
  the basis of a contract between the employer and the preferred
  supplier for the required work.

Single-stage tendering is appropriate where the employer's
requirements for the work are sufficiently developed so that a firm
price, with accompanying proposals, if any, for how any design is to
be completed, can be given for carrying out the required

works. Two-stage tendering may be appropriate where the employer's requirements are not sufficiently developed to invite tenders for the execution of the works, and it wishes to obtain the expertise of a preferred supplier in developing those requirements to a stage where a tender can be invited for their construction. Since it is possible that the successful first-stage tenderer will not be successful at the second stage, it is important that the first-stage tender documents make clear that the employer has the right to engage others to carry out the work as developed by the successful first-stage tenderer.

Whichever system of tendering is used, the tender documents should identify the criteria that will be used in assessing tenders, while making it clear that the employer need not accept any of the tenders it receives. Once received, tenders should be evaluated in the light of the stated criteria. The results of this evaluation should be recorded to minimise the risk that a dissatisfied tenderer can contend that the employer failed, in breach of the contract created by the tender process, to properly consider its tender.

7.4 Contracting procedures for employer-designated subcontractors

There may be circumstances in which the employer, or its advisers, want part of the work to be carried out by a subcontractor engaged for that purpose by the main contractor. If so, this must be made clear in the tender documentation for the main contract and provided for in the proposed terms of contract. An example of such provisions can be found in the naming provisions of the JCT Intermediate Form of Contract and in the nomination provisions in the JCT Standard Form of Building Contract.

Both of these standard forms envisage that a preferred designated subcontractor and its price for the relevant part of the work will be identified by the employer or its advisers, whether by direct negotiation or by competitive tender, and that the price for that part of the work will be identified in the main contract documents as a **prime cost sum**, as required by the Standard Method of

. Both standard forms require the designated
..tor to be engaged using the standard terms of
..tract published by the Joint Contracts Tribunal for that
..rpose, and identify a number of ancillary documents that are to
be used in tendering for and engaging the designated subcontractor.
It is important that none of these ancillary forms is overlooked.

- Quotations for employer-designated subcontract work should be
  invited using the relevant standard form of tender (NSC/T for the
  Standard Form, NAM/T for the Intermediate Form). This ensures
  that the mechanisms and terms on which the subcontract will be
  concluded are brought to the attention of those quoting for the
  work. When programming tender procedures for designated
  subcontract work, it should be borne in mind that both NSC/T
  and NAM/T require the insertion of information concerning the
  proposed terms of the main contract that may not be available
  until the main contract tender documentation is prepared.
- If NAM/T is used, and the subcontractor is to provide a warranty
  to the employer, this requirement should be expressly stated, and
  the terms of the warranty identified, since the Joint Contracts
  Tribunal does not provide a standard form warranty, equivalent to
  NSC/W, for use with the Intermediate Form. The Royal Institute
  of British Architects and the Specialist Engineering Contractors
  Group publish a warranty, ESA/1, for this purpose. If this warranty
  is to be used, a copy should be provided to tenderers, at the latest
  when they are invited to tender on the terms of NAM/T.
- Once the main contractor is engaged, it should be instructed to
  enter into a contract with the designated subcontractor on the
  subcontract terms provided for in the main contract (NSC/C and
  NSC/A for the Standard Form, NAM/SC and the copy of NAM/T
  completed by the subcontractor for the Intermediate form).
  Where the instruction is issued under the Standard Form, the
  standard form NSC/N should be used. The Joint Contracts
  Tribunal does not publish a standard form instruction for use
  with the Intermediate Form.
- Once the subcontract is in place, the subcontractor should be
  instructed to execute a warranty in the employer's favour in the

applicable terms (NSC/W for the Standard Form; the agreed form of warranty, usually ESA/1, for the Intermediate Form). The warranty must be executed promptly. Until it is in place, the employer has no recourse against the subcontractor if it fails to perform its work properly. This is particularly important if the work includes design, since the employer has no recourse against the main contractor for defects in that design.

Although these procedures may seem unduly complex and are, of course, applicable only to procurement under the JCT Standard Form of Building Contract and Intermediate Form, they highlight a number of matters that must be addressed whenever employer-designated subcontracts are proposed.

- How is the relevant part of the works to be described? When, and on what terms, is a quotation to be obtained for that work and a preferred subcontractor identified?
- Does the main contract entitle the employer to designate a subcontractor to carry out a part of the main contract work who must then be engaged by the contractor for that part of the work?
- Does the main contract identify the terms on which the subcontract is to be concluded and provide for what is to happen if the designated subcontractor will not contract with the main contractor or, having done so, fails to complete the work because, for instance, of insolvency or default?
- Must the main contractor be instructed to subcontract with the designated subcontractor or is it obliged to do so under the terms of the main contract without the need for a specific instruction?
- Is the designated subcontractor to provide a warranty to the employer with respect to the performance of some or all of its obligations and, if so, on what terms? A warranty is essential if there is any doubt about whether the main contractor, when appointed, will be liable for all of the work carried out by the designated subcontractor, for example where the designated subcontractor is a specialist providing design as well as construction, or where part of the designated subcontractor's work is completed before the main contractor is engaged.

s are not addressed, the employer may be exposed to
, in the event of non-performance or defective
nance by the designated subcontractor, than would otherwise
ne case. In particular, the employer may not be able to recover
losses due to such non-performance or defective performance from
either the main contractor or the designated subcontractor.

7.5 Contracting procedures for public bodies and utilities

There are various statutory provisions that give effect to European
Union Directives governing the manner in which certain contracts
are procured by public bodies and utilities. These are works
contracts with a value (current at the date of this publication)
exceeding €5 million and supply or services contracts with a value
(current at the date of this publication) exceeding either €130,000
or €200,000, depending on the circumstances. Public bodies include
government departments, local authorities, government agencies,
hospital trusts, state schools and the like. Utilities include water,
energy, transport and telecommunication utility companies.

The requirements that must be observed include the following.

- Intended contracts must be advertised in the prescribed manner
  in the *Official Journal of the European Community*.
- Specifications must, where possible, give preference to European
  standards and must not discriminate against contractors,
  suppliers or service providers from other member countries of
  the European Union. Specifications should not, unless this is
  unavoidable, refer to particular suppliers or products, and then
  only if words are added to make clear that equivalent suppliers
  or products will be acceptable.
- Public bodies should ordinarily use an open or restricted tender
  procedure complying with the statutory requirements and must
  award tenders to either the lowest or, if this criteria is identified
  in the tender documents, the most economically advantageous
  tender. The negotiated procedure can only be used in exceptional
  circumstances.

- Utilities have greater flexibility over whether to use open, restricted or negotiated tender procedures.

7.6 Concluding a contract with a preferred supplier

The manner in which a contract is concluded with a preferred supplier depends principally on whether the contract is to be executed as a deed or not, and on whether a standard form contract is to be used and, if so, what matters have to be agreed before a contract on those terms can be concluded.

Where a standard form contract is used, the temptation to amend its terms should be resisted unless competent legal advice is obtained and the need for such amendments is clearly established. At best, bespoke amendments add an additional layer of complexity and uncertainty to any disputes that may arise between the parties. At worst, they make the standard terms unworkable.

7.6.1 Contracts for consultants' services

Where, as is often the case, a consultant's appointment with its client is to be concluded on the standard terms published by its professional body, the following matters should be considered.

- Almost all standard form consultants' agreements require the parties to agree certain matters identified in schedules to the terms, such as client's brief, scope of services and basis of fees. If these matters are not agreed and recorded in the contract, the contract or certain of its terms may fail for uncertainty.
- If documents other than the standard form are to be included in the contract, these should be expressly identified by appropriate entries in the standard form or in the correspondence by which the contract is to be formed.
- Almost all standard form consultants' agreements include exemption and limitation clauses, some of which may need to be specifically selected by entry in the relevant appendix or schedule to the terms. If these clauses are not drawn to the client's attention and openly negotiated, and the information

necessary to complete the related appendix entries identified in the contract, such clauses may be unenforceable.

- Many standard form consultants' agreements provide for a variety of different methods of dispute resolution. These should be discussed with the client, and any information required by the selected options (such as the identity of any appointing bodies for arbitrators or adjudicators) should be identified in the contract. If the client is a consumer, rather than a business, an appointing body other than the consultant's professional body should be considered. A clause that provides for disputes with the consultant to be resolved by a person appointed by the consultant's professional body might well be regarded as unfair under the Unfair Terms in Consumer Contracts Regulations. If the proposed contract concerns work for a residential occupier on their own home, the desirability or otherwise of retaining the adjudication provision should be considered with the client since there is no statutory requirement for such a provision. If this is not done, the provision is likely to be invalid against the consumer under the Unfair Terms in Consumer Contracts Regulations.

If the contract is to be concluded by signing a standard form one, preferably two, originals of the form together with any incorporated documents should be prepared with the schedule and appendix entries, if any, completed. To avoid later disputes about what was agreed, the parties should initial manuscript entries in the form and the incorporated documents, if any, at the time of execution. If the contract is to be made by deed, care should be taken to ensure that the correct formalities are used. If two originals are prepared, then both should be signed and initialled, with each party retaining a signed original. If one original is prepared for signature, one party should keep the original and the other given a copy.

If the contract is to be concluded by letter, whether signed by both parties or not, the letter should clearly and unambiguously identify any standard terms on which the contract is based. It should highlight any exemption or exclusion clauses in those terms, including the dispute resolution clauses, and record the outcome of any discussions between the parties concerning those clauses. The letter should also identify all the information that would have had to be inserted in the schedules and appendix to those terms, if any, had a copy of those terms to be signed by the parties. This should be done by setting out that information in the letter itself or in a schedule referred to in the letter and enclosed with it.

If the consultant is to be appointed on the client's terms, similar considerations apply. The consultant should review, with his insurers if necessary, the proposed terms for any obligations that extend beyond that of skill and care or which create liabilities to persons other than the client. If such provisions are insisted upon, the consultant should ensure that the associated risks are reflected in its fees and properly managed.

7.6.2 Subcontracts for consultants' services
The two situations in which subcontracts for consultant services are most commonly used are where a design and build contractor engages a subconsultant to complete the design that the contractor is obliged to provide under the main contract, and where a consultant engages a subconsultant to carry out part of the services that the consultant is to provide under its contract with the client.

If the subcontract incorporates a standard form consultant's agreement, similar considerations apply as when a consultant is appointed by a client. But, since the consultant is a subconsultant, the matters that must be considered where a subcontractor is engaged should also be borne in mind. Similar considerations apply where the subcontract with the consultant is not on standard terms.

7.6.3 Main contracts for construction works
Where, as will usually be the case, a main contract for construction works is to be concluded on a standard form, the following matters should be considered.

- Many standard form construction contracts include alternative provisions that have to be selected and entries that have to be completed, either by making the appropriate alterations to the standard terms or by completing an appendix identifying such matters. If the required matters are not agreed and recorded in the contract, the contract or the affected terms may fail for uncertainty.

- Some standard form contracts contain a variety of optional supplements such as supplements providing for phased (sectional) completion, and forms such as bonds and warranties. Any options or entries required by such supplements and forms should be agreed and recorded in the contract, otherwise they may, because of uncertainty, fail to be properly incorporated.
- Where the contract is prepared by a consultant on behalf of a client, the terms and the implications of any alternatives or insertions required by the terms should be discussed and agreed with the client before tenders, if any, are invited and a contractor engaged. Of particular concern are provisions that require the employer to carry insurance, since the availability of such insurance and its cost must be established before tenders are invited. Also of concern are provisions for dispute resolution; particularly in the case of domestic clients, adjudication. Adjudication is not a statutory requirement in a construction contract entered into with an individual for work on their home and it may not be appropriate in such a contract.
- Most standard form contracts are periodically amended by the body responsible for their preparation, by issue of amendment sheets. Care should be taken to ensure that the latest amendment sheets are incorporated, unless there is a specific reason why they should not be.
- All standard form construction contracts provide for documents describing the work, and its price, to be incorporated into the contract. It is important that such documents are clearly and unambiguously identified either by appropriate entries in the standard form or, if the contract is to be concluded by letter, in the correspondence by which the contract is to be concluded.
- Many standard form construction contracts include a provision that gives priority to the standard terms in the event of conflicts between the standard terms and terms included in documents,

such as the drawings, preliminaries and specification, specially prepared for the project. The effect of such a provision may be to invalidate amendments or additions to the standard terms set out in the specially prepared contract documents. For such amendments and additions to be effective, they should be identified in the standard form itself, either by amending the affected terms or by adding a provision that identifies and incorporates a schedule in which the amendments can be found.

- Almost all standard form construction contracts provide for a variety of different methods of dispute resolution. Any information required by the selected options, such as the identity of appointing bodies, should be identified in the contract.

Many standard form construction contracts provide an attestation section that the parties can execute to conclude the contract. If the contract is to be executed one, preferably two, copies of the standard form, including any supplements and standard forms, and the competed appendix, if any, should be prepared together with the same number of copies of the incorporated documents such as drawings, bills and specifications. To avoid later disputes about what was agreed, manuscript entries in the standard form and the copies of the incorporated documents should be initialled by both parties at the time of execution. If the contract is to be made by deed, care should be taken to ensure that the correct formalities are used.

If the contract is to be concluded by letter, whether signed by both parties or not, the letter should clearly and unambiguously identify the standard terms on which the contract is based and, if not clear from the standard form itself, all of the supplements, forms, amendment sheets and documents to be incorporated. In most cases one of the incorporated documents (usually the preambles to the specification or bills) will identify, in the case of any optional terms in the standard form, which have been selected and will set out any insertions required by terms of the standard form, such as commencement and completion dates. If this is not the case, this information should be set out in the correspondence by which the contract is to be concluded.

7.6.4 Subcontracts for construction work

Subcontracts for construction work are formed either on the basis of standard terms of subcontract that are compatible with the standard form main contract which they concern, or on the basis of 'in-house' terms proposed by the subcontractor or, more usually, the contractor. Contracts of the latter type are frequently encountered where subcontractors, in turn, engage others to perform part of their work.

In some cases the contractor may be obliged under the main contract to engage the subcontractor using a specific standard form of subcontract or to include specific provisions in the subcontract. If so, the required standard forms or provisions should be used.

If a standard form subcontract is used, similar considerations apply to those that apply where a standard form main contract is concluded. If the contract is to be concluded on the basis of the contractor's or subcontractor's in-house terms, it is important that these are included with or identified in the letter of offer along with all of the other documents to be included in the subcontract.

In either case, particular care should be taken over the following matters.

- The work to be supplied under the subcontract should mirror the equivalent part of the contractor's works under the main contract. This is usually done by identifying relevant extracts from the main contract drawings and specifications as subcontract documents.
- The contract period for the subcontract work should reflect the programme to which the contractor is working.
- If the contractor is obliged to provide information about the subcontract work to the employer, there should be similar obligations on the subcontractor in the subcontract. This is particularly important where the subcontractor's work includes a design element.
- If the main contract obliges the contractor to include specific

terms in the subcontract, or requires the contractor to procure warranties or bonds from the subcontractor, this should be reflected in the terms of the subcontract.

• If the main contract includes provisions that entitle one or other party to determine or suspend its obligations or those of the other party, any such determination or suspension should also apply under the subcontract. If this is not done, the exercise of such rights under the main contract may, by preventing the subcontractor performing its work, be a breach of the subcontract by the contractor.

• It is advisable to make a copy of the main contract available to the subcontractor for inspection so that the subcontractor is aware, before it is engaged, of liabilities that the main contractor will incur if the subcontract works are not properly performed.

• If the main contract is executed as a deed then, ideally, the subcontract should also be executed as a deed.

7.6.5 Bonds and warranties

Since the obligation to provide a warranty or bond will be unenforceable for uncertainty unless the terms of the warranty or bond are agreed at the time the contract creating the obligation to provide the warranty or bond is concluded, the terms of the warranty or bond (including any options or insertions provided for in those terms) must be set out or incorporated by reference into that contract. If the warranty is to be executed as a deed, this should also be stated.

Standard form warranties are published by bodies such as the British Property Federation, and the Joint Contracts Tribunal publishes a variety of warranties and bonds for use with specific provisions of its standard form contracts. Banks and insurance companies provide standard wording for bonds, but these have to be treated with caution since they may not be suitable, without modification, for use on construction projects.

Since the wording of the warranty or bond is, ordinarily, predetermined under the contract with the party giving the warranty, the subsequent preparation of the relevant document and its execution is usually a mechanical exercise.

Appendix 1. Further reading

For a more detailed consideration of the law of contract see the most recent edition of a good student textbook, such as:

- Poole, J, *Textbook on contract law*, Blackstone, London.
- Furmston, M P et al, *Cheshire, Fifoot and Furmston's law of contract*, Butterworths, London.

For a less weighty consideration of the law of contract see, for example:

- Speaight, A and Stone G, *The architect's legal handbook*, 7th edition, 2000, Architectural Press, Oxford; particularly Chapters 1, 2, 8 and 29.
- Uff, J, *Construction law: law and practice relating to the construction industry*, 2002, 8th edition, Sweet & Maxwell, London; particularly Chapters 1, 4–8 and 10.

For a discussion of practical issues concerning contract formation see, for example:

- Lupton, S, *Architect's job book*, 7th edition, 2000, RIBA Publications Ltd; particularly Parts PRE-AG and G.
- Cox, S and Clamp, H, *Which contract? Choosing the appropriate building contract*, 3rd edition, 2003, RIBA Enterprises.

For guidance on contract procedures see, for example:

- *Engaging an Architect: Guidance for Clients on Quality Based Selection*, Construction Industry Council & RIBA, 1999, RIBA Publications.
- *Engaging an Architect: including guidance on fees*, Updated April 2000, RIBA, 2000, RIBA Companies Ltd.
- National Joint Consultative Committee for Building, *Code of procedure for selective tendering for design and build*, 1995, RIBA Publications Ltd, London.
- National Joint Consultative Committee for Building, *Code of*

procedure for single stage selective tendering, 1996, RIBA Publications Ltd, London.
- National Joint Consultative Committee for Building, *Code of procedure for two stage selective tendering*, 1996, RIBA Publications Ltd, London.

For the impact of European law on contract procurement, see:

- Dalby, J, *EU law for the construction industry*, 1998, Blackwell Science, Oxford.

Appendix 2. Relevant legislation

Note: Most of the legislation referred to below can be accessed thorough the HMSO web site at *www.hmso.gov.uk*.

Terms implied by statute
The principal statues that imply terms into contracts for the sale of goods, the supply of goods and the supply of goods and services are:

The Sale of Goods Act 1979, as amended;
The Supply of Goods (Implied Terms) Act 1973, as amended;
The Supply of Goods and Services Act 1982, as amended.

Statutory controls over exemption clauses
The principal statutory controls over exemption clauses are found in:

The Unfair Contracts Terms Act 1977, as amended;
The Unfair Terms in Consumer Contracts Regulations 1999
(SI 1999/2083).

Dispute resolution
The principal legislation relevant to dispute resolution in the construction industry is:

The Housing Grants, Construction and Regeneration Act 1996, Part II;
The Scheme for Construction Contracts (England and Wales)
Regulations 1998 (SI 1998/649);
The Construction Contracts (England and Wales) Exclusion Order
1998 (SI 1998/648);
The Arbitration Act 1996.

Procurement of public works
The principal legalisation governing the procurement of public works is:

The Public Works Contracts Regulations 1991 (SI 1991/2680),
as amended;

The Public Services Contracts Regulations 1993 (SI 1993/3228),
as amended;
The Public Supply Contracts Regulations 1995 (SI 1995/201),
as amended;
The Utility Contracts Regulations 1996 (SI 1996/2911),
as amended.

The Government publishes a number of technical notes concerning
this legislation which, although not of legislative force, provide
guidance about its operation. These are available from HM Treasury,
Public Enquiry Unit, Room 89/2, Treasury, Parliament Street, London
SWIP 3AG.